Pamela Letitia

Enjoy!

Imagine!

Great to have played in the flute section of CCCB with you, Sue!

Friend —
Anne Crans

Pictured Life

And True Stories from Northern and Upper Michigan

Anneke Letitia Van Ooyen Crans

Copyright © 2023 Anneke Letitia Van Ooyen Crans.

All rights reserved. No part of this book may be used or reproduced by any means, graphic, electronic, or mechanical, including photocopying, recording, taping or by any information storage retrieval system without the written permission of the author except in the case of brief quotations embodied in critical articles and reviews.

This book is a work of non-fiction. Unless otherwise noted, the author and the publisher make no explicit guarantees as to the accuracy of the information contained in this book and in some cases, names of people and places have been altered to protect their privacy.

Archway Publishing books may be ordered through booksellers or by contacting:

Archway Publishing
1663 Liberty Drive
Bloomington, IN 47403
www.archwaypublishing.com
844-669-3957

Because of the dynamic nature of the Internet, any web addresses or links contained in this book may have changed since publication and may no longer be valid. The views expressed in this work are solely those of the author and do not necessarily reflect the views of the publisher, and the publisher hereby disclaims any responsibility for them.

Any people depicted in stock imagery provided by Getty Images are models, and such images are being used for illustrative purposes only.
Certain stock imagery © Getty Images.

Interior Image Credit: Anneke Letitia Van Ooyen Crans

Scripture quotations taken from The Holy Bible, New International Version® NIV® Copyright © 1973 1978 1984 2011 by Biblica, Inc. TM. Used by permission. All rights reserved worldwide.

ISBN: 978-1-6657-2864-5 (sc)
ISBN: 978-1-6657-2866-9 (hc)
ISBN: 978-1-6657-2865-2 (e)

Library of Congress Control Number: 2022915185

Printed in the United States of America.

Archway Publishing rev. date: 06/12/2023

Dedicated to my computer-tech, adopted, Korean brother,
Thank-you!

Wisdom, Intelligence, Love
Always ready to help

John Kim Van Ooyen

Contents

North Bessemer School 1
Opening the Door 3
Tomorrow is my birthday; I will be five years old. 3
Wisdom 6
Pathway Of Wildflowers 7
Oaken Door 8
Light Shining 10
Delicious Red Apples 14
Viewing the School 15
North Bessemer School 16
Class Bully 18
Finn School 19
The Bathroom 20
North Bessemer School 22
The Home of the North Bessemer School Principal 24
Hedberg Barn 1912 25
Hedberg House 1912 26
Hedberg Family House 1920 27
Privileged Children 32
The Orange-belted Bumblebee 34
Under the Old Oak Tree 36
Spring Life Flowers 37
The Red Rose 38
Grandfather 40
The Bald Eagle Watches 41
Eel Lake Loons 43
Imagine Truth 45
Yellow Bumblebee 46
Today Is My Birthday; I Am Eight Years Old 48
Sandhill Cranes 50
My Mother, Amy J. Van Ooyen 54
Books 55
Stories 56
Pathways 57
Bessemer 59
My Father, Claude Van Ooyen, the Organist 61

Today Is My Birthday; I Am Eleven Years Old.	62
Pathway Blooms	63
The Barn	65
Barn of Agate Beach Road	68
First Settlers—Central Lower Michigan	69
Western Lower Peninsula Michigan	70
Jamestown	71
Byron Center	72
Farm House Highway 117	75
Insects Flowering	76
Wolf Spider	77
Life Cycle	78
Central Lower Peninsula	79
First Settlers—Yellow Home	80
Byron Center	81
West Baldwin, Jenison	82
South Grandville	83
Life Promised	84
Immigrants	85
The Organ—the Piano	86
First Settlers	87
Allegan	88
South Grandville	88
Shell Barn	90
Shell Barn US 2	92
Alba, Michigan	93
Allendale Homestead	95
Seagull Flight	96
Gross Cap Village	97
Delicious Red Apples	101
Pewabic Village	102
Treasure	103
Ramsey High School	104
Ramsey High School—Ramsey Village	105
Ramsey High School	107
Cornerstone Cross 1921–1923	108
Home—Hope—Cousins	110
Family	111
The Fire	112
Camp Tent City	113
Northwest Ironwood	120
Spring	123
Today is my birthday; I am thirteen years old.	123
Fern School Dist. No. 3 CW.1906	124
Lake City	126
Highway 20 First Settlers	128

Ironwood Episcopalian Church	129
Covington Catholic Church	130
Eden Dist. No 2. 1892	133
First Settlers	135
Western Upper Peninsula	135
Van Ooyen Family	137
Table for Eleven plus Two	140
Ontonagon	142
Ontonagon	143
Poor Farm Homestead	144
Red Truck	145
Tender Love	146
Apple Tree Blossoms	148
Jamestown Rural School	149
Alba Hotel Bar	151
Rejoicing	153
Pathway	154
Red Chevy Truck—1953	155
Covington Catholic Church	158
Yellow Home	159
First Settlers	160
Lake Superior—Indian Maiden	161
Indian Maiden	162
Oman's Blue House	163
Little Girls Point	165
Home of the Pastor	166
Tunnel Collapse—1926	172
Cliff Copper Mine	173
Hoekstra-Van Ooyen Cabin	176
Gosling Feather	179
Reflection	180
Highlight Photos	184
On Golden Pond	185
Transition	186
River of Life	187
Champion Mine # 4	188
Copper Range-Painesdale Keweenaw Peninsula, Michigan	189
Quincy Mine	190
Lake Superior Shoreline	191
Little Girls Point County Park	192
Coopersville & Marne Train	193
Acknowledgements	198

Prologue

Promises and hope—the immigrant seeks. Homes, barns, and schools were built with hope. Light became hope. Apple trees were planted. Fertile ground and fresh sweet water gave opportunity. Copper was discovered. The Upper Peninsula of Michigan flourished as families raised their children with wisdom and hope.

    Remnants remain. The stories are recorded by Anne. Stories, intertwined with visual brilliance, of friendly, furiously independent people of the Upper Peninsula of the state of Michigan.

    Come into my world—imagine—sit by a warm fire. Imagine the life that was once lived. View the photos; read the stories. View the beauty; feel the struggles of the immigrants—Finns, Norwegians, Welsh, Germans, Italians, and Poles.

Great Horned Owl

My eyes lift upward
I listen as I view
The sound of birds above
Drawn into my ears

My eyes view colors of green
Among and below the trees I lay
Bird calls become clarity
I hear the Cardinal

The call of the Goldfinch
The caw of the Blackbird
The tap of the Downy Woodpecker
The loud distant tap of the Pileated Woodpecker

The evening call of the Loon I hear
Bullfrogs sound their desperate evening croaks
High above, the Nightingale sooths my soul
After the clock strikes twelve …

I tune into the wisdom of the Great Horned Owl
I have returned
I heard the Great Owl speak

Wisdom

North Bessemer School Promises

The Light Welcomes You

Door handle—through a window crack, I peer

Light—sunbeams through cracks of pane

Light—green summer ferns densely growing

Vines encumbered, vines of light, growing upward, around, and through, entangled

Light above, I see the filament, the bulb, and the pale green fixture cover

The piano, the organ, the stringed tones, I hear voices

I hear the flute

I see the eyes of the children
I listen to the voices of the children
Singing

Light caught my eye
Door handle remains, a firm grip—I see light
I open the door

Light remains shining, wisdom for the children

Children, of the light, I see
Light forever

Light for all

Children

Future

Opening the Door

Tomorrow is my birthday; I will be five years old.

The brass door handle leads to a new life.

Quietly, I walk upon the pathway. I look upward and gaze at the enormous oak door. Along my pathway, I see wild flowers. In anxious excitement, I reach upward to open the ancient, dark-stained, hardwood door.

The yellow black-eyed Susan daisies watch me. A painted lady butterfly views my every movement. I see the lock on the handle of the door; I open it. The great horned owl of wisdom watches as hope is given to me. Hope is the wisdom of my forefathers. I am at reverent peace, as I will study, and I will learn by doing my best always.

The window above me sees me and reveals my classroom. I walk in with silent reverence. I feel divine presence. I will be blessed.

I peek into my classroom. My thoughts wander—thoughts of past and thoughts of present. I see the lights hanging below the structure of the strong oak beams. Strength is present—the strength of my forefathers. Strength of thought, strength of mind, and strength of body—I am blessed was my thought.

The perseverance of the forefathers was passed to the children, as they learned at North Bessemer School.

The great horned owl cares and blesses—knowing all.

Window Pane Crack Opening

Pathway Of Wildflowers

Oaken Door Panes Cracked Light Enters

Light Shining

Light

North Classroom

South Classroom

Delicious Red Apples

I see shiny, bright red, wild delicious red apples climbing the North Bessemer School building; I take a closer look. I will bring my kind, intelligent teacher—a delicious red apple.

Oh, how she loved the bright red color, the fragrance, and the taste.

Delicious Red Apples

Viewing the School

Blessed is North Bessemer School, built on a hilltop. I see that a maple tree was planted, which is now fully grown. Growing as I grow—tall, outstretched, and somewhat spindly, but maturing. This is the gift to me from my days at North Bessemer School.

Many days pass. I grow. Many children have pursued knowledge in the North Bessemer School. The classrooms were filled; two large classrooms, for grades K through three, an auditorium was built on the north side of the school.

My favorite room of North Bessemer School was the auditorium. All students would stand on the stage and sing favorite songs chosen by our teachers. The entire community would look forward to celebrative concert events: fall, Christmas, Easter, and grandparent programs. My teacher placed me in the front row: I was short. "Away in the Manger," "Silent Night"— all my favorite songs were on this Christmas program. Four teachers lived on the second floor of the school, foresight of our forefathers.

Directly behind North Bessemer School was a home built by first immigrants from Finland, the Hedberg family. The Hedberg family first immigrated in 1902 on their honeymoon, which followed a return to Finland; immigrating a second time in 1912 with seven children. With five more children born in America, a blessing of twelve children—six boys and six girls, with two sets of twins, a new home was built in 1920 on Hedberg Road. North Bessemer School was built on the corner of Hedberg Road and Sandene Road.

One winter day in 1938, the snow began to fall. A blizzard, it was, they said. Oh my, we were stranded. Blizzard winds caused drifts of twenty-five feet—my teacher measured the depth. People of the Bessemer community walked in the snow, not realizing they were walking on top of cars and homes. Men, women, and children dug tunnels through the snow in order to traverse from one place to another. The temperature was minus 33 F. History records fifty people across Upper Peninsula died as a result of this blizzard.

We were cold, and we were hungry. We huddled together. And we became anxious. We began to bicker.

North Bessemer School
Facing East

North Bessemer School
Facing West

Class Bully

The tall bully of the class walked up to me. He stared into my eyes and then gave me a shove. He was burly, with dark-black hair. His eyes were not happy.

I became very anxious. I cried. I was cold, and I was hungry. We all were cold and hungry. My wonderful, kind, and beautiful teacher calmed me and the other students.

Forty-three students were in our classroom. We huddled tenderly around our teacher. We listened to the gentle voice of our teacher as she sang "Silent Night." We felt calm. Then she took a favorite book from the classroom library shelf and read to us. The book was *Little Women* by Louisa May Alcott

This is a story I will always remember.

A best friend and neighbor, Dave, joined the classrooms of North Bessemer School. The school of a nearby village, Ironwood, had too many students. Therefore, a recommendation was given for many children to attend North Bessemer School. Dave was cold and stranded too. He was in grade three.

After six days, we were rescued. An uncle of several of the students, Uncle Tauno, came with his team of horses harnessed to a long, wide sleigh to pick us up. All the students were rescued and brought home in his sleigh. The sleigh had enclosed sides and a rail with small windows to peek through. The horses, covered in ice and snow, were dark auburn brown, sleek and beautiful. I could see the frozen breath of the horses in the minus thirty-three-degree temperature. The snow drifts were twenty-five feet deep. Four horses pulled the sleigh.

My large, dark brown eyes saw everything. It was snowing with whipping winds blowing through the tiny windows. Brightly colored blankets were wrapped around each one of us. I was given a bright red, soft, wool lambskin blanket. My teacher wrapped the blanket around my neck and face. I could peek through a tiny window.

My favorite color is red—I still have the blanket.

I will remember forever, the blizzard of 1938.

I will never forget.

—if you could only imagine—

Finn School

School Garage 1930

The Bathroom

The guys had a bathroom on the left, and the gals on the right, with a special room for the smelly other. Being very, very shy, I was so thankful for the privacy.

Two sinks—the smaller, lower sink was my size. When I had to wash my hands, it fit. I was short and petite with long wispy, curly-blond hair.

I was careful not to drip water on the floor. Slowly, I washed my hands. I see the paper towel dryer.

I dried my hands.

Lights

I see lights still hanging; the bulb, the filament a stark reminder of light.

I remember when the lights went out. It was dark, and the heater no longer worked. After the second night, we had run out of coal for the furnace.

I touched the radiator. It was cold.

Oh my, what a memory! I will never forget how cold and frightened I was. How frightened we all were.

—if one could only imagine—

Guys and Gals Lavatories

North Bessemer School

Look at my beautiful North Bessemer School—it stands with pride and is filled with memories. The foresight of our forefathers became truth—their wisdom for their dearly beloved children. We were all loved, and we were all cherished. The maple tree grows.

    I felt loved.

Maple Tree
North Bessemer School

The Home of the North Bessemer School Principal

I see large rooms with windows facing the direction of the children in the school yard. The wife of our principal stood by her window every day watching the children play on the playground behind the school. Often, she would give us a wave. I looked out to see her smiling face. I could see the wrinkles at the corners of her mouth. Her friends called her Rose.

The design of the rooftop shingles utilized bright colors of green and red. They were the colors of red Lake Superior clay and a deep green color of the U.P. trees.

In the field, I observed a huge pile of hay stacked by hand in a row. The principal's family had cows and horses. The school children helped to bring in the hay and the straw for feed and bedding of the animals.

I loved the warm aroma of fresh hay.

The Children

Giggles
Laughter
Tag
Catch

Pencils
Paper
Desks
Books

Reading
Listening
Learning
Memorization

Wisdom

Hedberg Barn 1912

Hedberg House
First immigrant house
Family with seven children

Hedberg House 1912

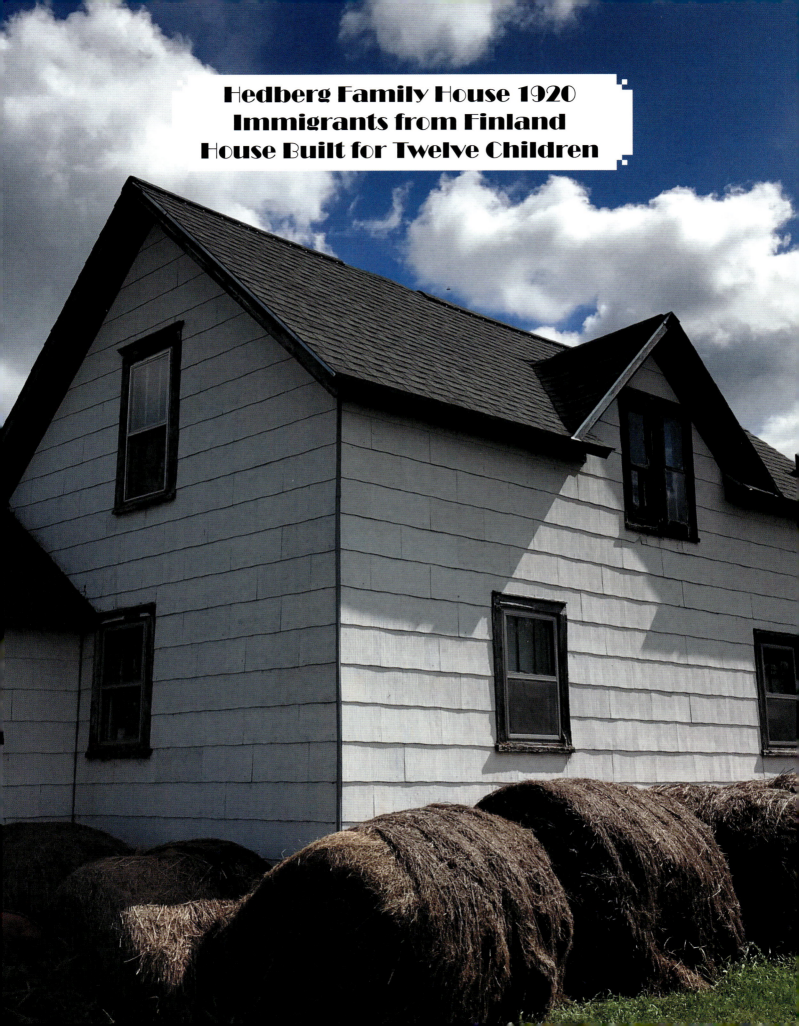

Hedberg Family House 1920
Immigrants from Finland
House Built for Twelve Children

120 Acres—the Corner Hedberg Family Land

Neighbors
First Settlers

Privileged Children

We were the privileged children—children of the classrooms, attending the beautiful school of North Bessemer. We had pride. When we gazed upward, we saw two large, wise owls at the entrance of the school building.

We were being educated. I knew this.

We thanked our moms and our dads for their wisdom, and always our God. We read from the Bible every morning, before our two-mile walk to school.

The dinner table was always filled with delicious warm foods: roasted meats, yellow Dutch potatoes, Dutch sliced green beans, fresh sweet corn, and applesauce with cinnamon topping. Our dessert most often was homemade pudding with summertime canned peaches as a topping.

Every Saturday, we baked for Sunday lunch and for after-church time coffee. Crunchy, sugar-topped cookies were a favorite.

Often, my best friend would join our family in baking and tasting the sugar cookies. Sugar cookies were her favorite.

On Saturday mornings, my mom made fluffy white bread—baking more than enough bread for the following week. The breads were placed in front of our four-legged wood stove; the warmth of the stove causing the yeasted bread to rise.

Eleven polished and shined pairs of shoes were lined up—it was my job, with my eldest sister, to polish the shoes every Saturday evening.

Stored on top of the stove—pan covers, with the pots and pans nearby, were piled twelve inches high. Sometimes the pile of pan covers would tip.

I can still hear the noisy clatter. Oh, the noise frightened me.

—if you could only imagine—

Wisdom

Orange-belted Bumblebee

Pathway

Yellow Bumblebee

Memorized

We memorized verses from the Bible, and we had to write them all down at semester's end. Eighteen verses in one semester, one for each week—a total of thirty-six for the school year.

I remember them all. Some of the assigned portions were several verses in length.

We sang the hymns, and memorized them all, too. Every morning our class would sing together. We had to sing loudly. We sang in tune. My teacher bent over and put his ear to our head to check if we were singing, and to listen if we were singing in tune.

I was shy and so embarrassed, as I know what "being in tune," is.

Now I chuckle; I am so happy and thankful for my forefathers ... and the education at the North Bessemer School.

The Orange-belted Bumblebee

I watched as the orange-belted bumblebee was sipping nectar from a giant, tall black-eyed Susan daisy. I loved all the wild flowers and all the insects. I remember all the flowers' and insects' names from when I was very young. My mom knew all the names too; I learned the names from my mom.

My mom and I would walk in the backyard—together we viewed the flowers, and watch the honeybees and bumblebees pollinate the flowers. I loved my mom.

My mom's yard was filled with red, yellow, white, blue, and purple flowers. My mom loved all the colors.

A favorite flower of my mom was the early spring, white lily of the valley. The lily of the valley flowers could be found in the shadows of the base of Oak trees.

—imagine—

Orange-belted Bumblebee

Spring Life Flowers

The Red Rose

The bright crimson red rose was my mom's very favorite color rose. My mom did not like mums.

My mom had received a cutting for this red rose from my grandfather. Her father lived in the Netherlands. On a return trip from visiting her parents in the Netherlands, my mom carried this red rose cutting gently wrapped inside her large, full-length, green wool coat pocket. This is how my mom brought her eye-catching, crimson red rose to the United States.

On a visit to the United States, my grandfather, Jacob Hoekstra, caught a large, twenty-five-inch fish in our neighborhood gypsum-mine quarry. The fish was a carp—bright orange and scaly. The carp was caught off a gypsum ledge in seventy feet deep water.

I touched the carp. The bright orange carp was slimy

I remember my grandfather's large smile. "Mooi" (beautiful), he said.

My mom made certain this large carp was planted under her red rose bush. I clearly remember the facial expressions my grandfather gave her. So disappointed he was, as he wanted to enjoy his fish for dinner that evening.

The red rose bloomed profusely every year. Neighbors came by "to take a peek." This rose was a standout as being the largest, most brilliant red rose in the neighborhood.

My *pake* ("grandfather") pruned the red rose.

My *beppe* ("grandmother") needed new dresses for the warmer climate of Michigan; my mom asked me to sew three dresses for my grandmother. One of the dresses required me to make a jacket to match. To keep me busy, was my mother's idea—my grandmother never wore the dresses after her return to her home country, the Netherlands. In asking why, my mom said the "style did not fit" in the Netherlands.

For six months, my *beppe* washed the dishes. "Kan ik U helpen?" (Can I help you?) She asked with a smile.

I smile with thankfulness. I feel an endearment.

I love my *beppe*.

—take time to imagine—

Grandfather
"Wat een mooi vissen!" (What a beautiful fish!)

The Bald Eagle Watches

"Watching over me," as the Bible says, this meaningful, gentle song I often sang in Sunday school.

I am excited and loved. The bald eagle flew above me. So does my story. I love telling you my story as I look up viewing the wing span of the eagle. Listening to the swish and swoosh of the wings, I felt the air movement.

Eel Lake

It was Sunday morning; I took my canoe out for a paddle. I viewed two loons flapping their strong wings, readying for flight to a warmer climate.

I watched the loons—a male and a female, as they were preening their feathers and testing the strength of their wings for the many miles ahead. I smile, as the young one could not yet fly.

The young loon would practice lifting out of the water many days before take-off several weeks later. In loon timing, the young loon would join the flight of a passing flock of loons.

My mom was the Eel Lake loon watcher and the questioner.

> Where did the Loons build their nest?
> Are the Loons being disturbed?
> How many chicks were hatched?
> How many chicks survived the summer?
> Did the Great Horned Owl steal a chick?
> Did the Bald Headed Eagle steal a chick?
> When did the young Loons take flight?

Sitting high in my canoe, I paddled among the loons. Watching the loons closely and looking downward over the aluminum edge of my canoe, I viewed two loons swimming alongside my canoe. Quickly, the loons disappeared, swimming beneath my canoe.

Where would the loons come up? I hold my breath, as I wait for the loons to resurface. Fifteen feet to my left two loons surfaced.

I view in amazement at the patterns of the feathers; a shimmering bright green neckband, with bright white feathers beneath. Silently, I paddled forward, so as not to disturb the loons, my soul being engulfed in total peace. My thought: *Am I dreaming?*

Bald Eagle

Eel Lake Loons

Imagine Truth

My grandfather is bringing in a last load of wood for the winter. My grandfather treasures his 1953, shiny, bright red Chevy truck. He is grateful! Sadly, the last load of cut oak wood did not get stacked.

    I am sad.

    My grandfather was killed as the tree fell on his back. The trunk of the tree fell across his strong back crushing his ribs. His heart stopped. The angle of his last cut was flawed, causing the tree trunk to fall prematurely—the load of wood remains on his truck to this day. I grieve for my grandfather still.

Do Not Cry

A giant Oak Tree
Branches spread
Leaves of dark brass green
Moss beneath

Memories of glory
Memories of delight
My children dance
My children say, "I love you, Grandpa."

One last limb
Taking a closer look
The spot is found
The cut is made

I hear a rumble
I am below
I cannot run
I crumble—upon the moss

Goodbye my children
I grieve for you
You grieve for me
I am perfection

"We Shall Meet Again"
"Oh, How He Loves You and Me"
"When the Roll Is Called up Yonder"
"I Love You, Lord"

Yellow Bumblebee

1953 Red Chevy Truck
Last Load

Today Is My Birthday; I Am Eight Years Old.

On this special day, my family planned a springtime trip to visit my grandparents. They lived in a very large farm house: six bedrooms, three bathrooms, a large family room, a kitchen, and a food-storage cellar.

A large porch straddled the front of the house. In the back of the house, an entry led to a basement cellar where food was stored. We cooked on an old iron wood-burning stove. Carefully preserved jars of peaches, tomatoes, applesauce, and green beans packed the basement shelves. Canned salmon and smelt filled jars on the upper shelf.

My grandparents' house was the first home built, and the largest, located on the east end of Upper Peninsula, Michigan. Being fortunate to immigrate with enough savings, carefully and painstakingly saved for the long trip to the United States, my grandparents were the first of our family to have emigrated from the Netherlands.

For two weeks, my grandparents traveled, crossing the ocean in a very large four-level boat—the *Rotterdam*. My grandparents, with their four children, the youngest a four-month-old baby, were assigned space on the lower level—a corner, with one small table and two bunk beds. A storm began to brew. Dark clouds encircled the boat—strong winds blew. I was four years old.

The storm was cause for panic, as the gigantic boat rolled back and forth with fury. Most of the passengers became miserably seasick. It was a cold, long, lonely boat crossing, of fifteen days, on the Atlantic Ocean, to travel to the United States of America. Upon arrival, everyone climbed to the deck. The sky was dark; it was windy and cold, as all passengers careened their heads to view the welcoming sight of the Statue of Liberty.

Morning porridge was not eaten.

We were a large family, and the Bible was read every day. Psalm 121 was my mom's favorite—"the traveling Psalm," my mom said. Every time we would leave for our home, my father would read Psalm 121, and he would pray for the safety of all his children. My grandfather led us in songs: "Blest Be the Tie that Binds," "Lord, Hear Your Children Praying," "Heavenly Sunshine," "He Leadeth Me," "Precious Lord." These were good times with our family of eleven children.

My grandfather took me on walks through fields of flowers—the Queen Anne's lace, white daisies, purple cone flowers, wild pink aster, and the lilies of the valley—my favorite. I love my memories. Inside the purple cone flower, I saw a yellow bumblebee.

—if you could only imagine—

Yellow Home

Sandhill Cranes

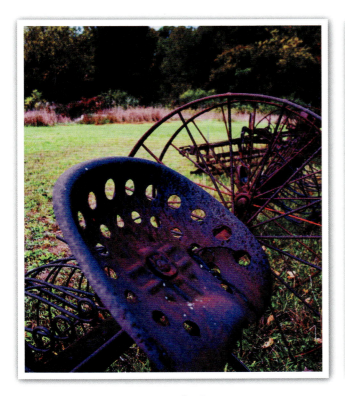
Purple Seat

Farm Implements

Sandhill Cranes

I love the sounds of the insects and the feel of the grasses. Large green crickets leaped in front of me. What fun! I will never forget! I even saw a Sandhill Crane, majestic and beautiful, preening. His mate was standing nearby—preening as well. They were doing their mating dance.

I see my grandfather's cow standing in my pathway.

Grandfather

My grandfather needed farm implements to gather the ripe hay and the tall, yellow, ready straw.
 I remember the perfect long rows. I see the implements of my grandfather: a rack, a plow, a cutter, a mower, a rake, a shovel, his wagon, and his pitchfork. I remember my grandfather leaning on his pitchfork.
 I loved the purple seat; sometimes I would sit on the big, cupped seat. Often, my grandfather would carry me on his shoulders, as we walked the pathway.
 I loved my grandfather.
 My grandfather worked furiously to bring in the yellow, ready straw before the rains would arrive.
 In the distance, I saw a farmer chop the head off a large rooster. The rooster lay on a large stump, held firmly by my grandfather, ready for the ax chop. The rooster ran around with his head cut off. I saw blood squirting. I saw the neck with no head. The rooster was large, a shiny, reddish-brown color.
 Oh, what a sight! I will never forget. I remain affright and aghast to this day.
 I tremble and shake.

—imagine—

Highway 28
Upper Peninsula, Michigan

Yellow Snapdragons ... Smiling in the Breezes ... Journey On

As yellow wildflower snap dragons nod, I am given direction to travel northeast;
I continue onward.

I find the sign, a sign in remembrance of Dr. Van Riper Sr. His name is engraved onto a copper plate in recognition of his love and civic duty to his community.

Within his garden I stood, assuring my walk, my journey. I am reminded of his life—dedication to his community, the village of Champion. Forever, he will be remembered and loved, for his dedicated life of service.

Dr. Van Riper gave a lifetime of healing and a life of service—for the creation of large and small creatures. The conservancy of nature he was witness to see and to live within.

A small camp on his favorite lake, Lake Michigamme, was where Dr. Van Ripper's nature's hideout, a one-room cedar log cabin, could be found. Only a few were privileged a visit to this special spot hidden within nature. My mom was privileged a visit. On the shoreline, she caught a large smallmouth bass—the largest bass she had ever caught. Dr. Van Riper took her picture holding the large bass.

The state park on Lake Michigamme is land donated to the State of Michigan by Dr. Van Riper Sr.

—can you imagine—

Lower Peninsula, Michigan　　　　　　　　　　**Pathways**

My Mother, Amy J. Van Ooyen

Dr. Van Riper Jr. was a mentor for my mom. My mom authored five books of short stories. Dr. Van Riper also encouraged my mom to publish these five books she wrote. The books were self-published; thousands were sold. Wow, I am so proud of my mom. Thus, my mom became famous in the Upper Peninsula of Michigan, Ironwood community, for her love of the U.P. people and love of all things created.

Amy Van Ooyen, lovingly, and tenderly spoken of, was well known as "Amy the Beekeeper" and "Amy the Author." Her legend, and her legacy, carries on through her five books throughout the Upper Peninsula of Michigan. She also was a representative and spoke for the Woman's Literary Club. Her voice was carried throughout an Upper Michigan circle. Her books were filled with true life encounters and non-fiction stories of her many friends in Upper Michigan.

Books authored by my mother, Amy J. Van Ooyen:

Creatures and Characters

Now and Then in the U.P.

Live it U.P.

A U.P. Dead End Road Never Ends

Transplants
An Immigration Encounter of East and West
Dutch Tulips & Oriental Poppies

Books
authored by Amy J. Hoekstra-Van Ooyen

Remembrance

Dr. Van Riper Sr.

Stories

One of the stories authored by my mom that comes to the forefront of my thought is of a dear elderly Native American Indian lady. I remember her deep, beautiful facial wrinkles. This dearly, respected lady was ninety-two years old. She kept a baby mouse between her breasts. "Must keep her warm," she said while sipping freshly brewed coffee and delighting in a taste of my mom's early-morning, freshly baked bread.

A slice of cinnamon apple cake was placed nearby her plate. "Take a peek," she said. I chuckled as I saw the whiskers, then the pointed nose, of a tiny, gray kangaroo mouse peek from between her warm hanging breasts. Yes, a warm spot to be nestled within.

Another story is about her friend from nearby Black River Harbor Road. Again, coffee time with my mom and her friend, as a spotted fawn shared kitchen space with us.

With clarity, I remember the hops the spotted fawn made around the kitchen table. Yes, my mom's friend had pity and a tender heart, with a curious resolution; the young fawn had "the run" inside of her home.

As I poured fresh thick cream into my coffee, the pink tongue of the young fawn quickly, silently gathered a lick.

Native American Indian

Respect
Warmth
Space

Mouse
Fawn
Coffee

Silence
Friend
Truth

Sharing
Love
Joy

Pathways

Watch Me "Moo"

Homestead
US 2
Upper Peninsula, Michigan

My Father, Claude Van Ooyen, the Organist

St. John's Lutheran Church

Covington Catholic Church

Today Is My Birthday; I Am Eleven Years Old.

My father, Claude Van Ooyen, was the organist of the Ironwood community. Most often, my father played for five churches in one weekend—two services on Saturday evening, and three services on Sunday morning.

On my visits, my father would take me along to play with him at the Christ Lutheran Church in Ironwood. I was invited to play my flute, accompanied by my father on the church pipe organ. Together, we played the prelude, offertory, postlude, and all the hymns sung by the congregants.

The Lutheran congregants sang meaningful hymns, composed in four-part musical arrangements, from the Lutheran Hymnal, "The Hymnal 1940."

A few of my favorite hymns:

"I Know My Faith Is Founded"
"Rock of Ages, Cleft for Me"
"Holy Spirit Hear Us"
"Hosanna, Lord Hosanna"

My father treated me to breakfast at a local restaurant in-between services—this is "what the Lutherans do," he commented.

I remember my father's serious, but mischievous, humorous facial expressions, along with a twinkle in his eyes.

My father was dedicated and talented; he was dearly loved by all. He was quiet, introspective, and a devoted religious man—highly respected by the churches in the U.P. for his deep thoughts and his music.

As I was waiting for the return train, I viewed the flowers. As I traveled, I was hypnotized by the colors and scent of the flowers.

In silence I journeyed in thoughts of His wonder, His beauty, and His creation.

Music filled my soul. I heard the sounds of Johann Sebastian Bach. I was privileged. I understood.

—can you imagine—

Pathway Blooms

Western Upper Peninsula

Marenisco Bridge, Highway 64

The Barn

In viewing the barn, with forty-eight milking cows and three horses working the fields, I smelled the sweat of the man: the father, my forefather, my grandfather.

I smelled the aroma of freshly-baked breads for the eleven children of the household. Many children, seventeen, were anticipated to join the children of our family for a Sunday afternoon lunch.

We sat around the enormous oak dining table. Oh my, Sunday noontime guests have arrived; the lively chatter rang in every corner of our spacious home.

I loved these times of friendship.

The Bible was opened to Psalm 121: 1-2, "I lift up my eyes to the hills—where does my help come from ... My help, cometh from the Lord, the Maker of heaven and earth" (NIV).

"Time to read the traveling Psalm," my mom said. "We must ask for protection of the children."

An extra leaf was placed on the table for our many guests—with respect, we listened, as my father read.

Twenty-three mouths to feed. This was Sunday lunch. Mom always prepared extra and many were blessed.

Games of hopscotch, tag, and jump rope were played in our large backyard after lunch.

A large, soft, red blanket was placed on the tender, lime-green grass to play games Old Maid and Uno. The family and guests were excited and happy; warm breezes blew, as beams of sunlight shone upon us.

As I continued to grow and learn—I remember well these days.

—if you can only imagine—

Early mornings, long hours ... empty pockets, and a strong back.

Elegance in design, the hope and the dreams, we gather, the family of eleven children. I remember the strong back of my father, his ribs protruding, the deep wrinkles, and the loose skin of an old man. Nickels were laid, in one long row, on the edge of the table; collection for the church—all for the poor, we were told. Our family had food aplenty, unfortunately newer immigrants—their tables were bare. My father and my mother were always willing to share.

Two years later, my father gave us quarters for the church collection. Our dining table was always ready for guests on Sunday, following the morning church service.

I am reminded of His goodness.

We ate together; my father read the Bible. We played games; the soft red blanket was spread on the grass—green soft luxurious, lime-colored grass, beneath the old oak tree.

Tall hardwood trees, maple and oak, shaded our backyard. The breezes were cool.

I smile as I remember my father's barn and the many barns of Upper and Lower Peninsulas of Michigan. Location, design, and color brought the barns to my view:

>Barn of Agate Beach Road
>Western Lower Peninsula
>Jamestown
>Byron Center
>Eastern Upper Lower Peninsula
>Barn on M 20
>Lake City
>Byron Center
>Barn on H 10
>Barn on US 2
>Barn on US 28
>Barn on Baldwin St.
>Barn on 32nd St.
>Barn on 84th St.
>Barn in Allegan

Barn of Agate Beach Road
Upper Peninsula, Michigan

First Settlers—Central Lower Michigan

Western Lower Peninsula Michigan

Jamestown
Lower Peninsula Michigan

Byron Center
Lower Peninsula Michigan

Eastern Upper Lower Peninsula, Michigan

Insects Flowering Beauty Design Surprise

Wolf Spider

I see a large wolf spider in the corner climbing the wall. I left nature to its own—I did not panic. I watched the quick jumps, jumps in rapid successive movements. Oh, what awkward progressions. The wolf spider jumped above my head. Looking upward, can I find the spider's web? Wandering into the barn and silo, our backyard insects, with amazing purpose and design, are revealed to me. Sitting on a pile of hay, I knew not to touch, as this wolf spider bites.

 I found the web.

Flowers and Butterflies

Lavender cone flowers nodded my direction. I love these flowers. Then I viewed the butterflies in bright colors. It was amazing. I know them all by name: painted lady butterfly, monarch butterfly, admiral butterfly, American butterfly, yellow tiger swallowtail, mourning cloak butterfly, summer azure moth, spicebush swallowtail butterfly, pipevine swallowtail butterfly, and pearl crescent—all drawing life from nectar and pollen of flowers.

 As I view, hope and promise is found.

Colors

Orange
Yellow
Red
Purple
Cream
Brown
Black
Life

—if you could only imagine—

Life Cycle

My father, now elderly, and my mother, no longer able to walk (she carried a stick, standing shakenly, severely hunched over, and tiny in stature), stood together on their house deck to give me a tender wave of welcome.

The silo and the barn of my parents could no longer be repaired. I wept in silence, and in thought, I pondered. Tears flowed from my eyes liberally, and rolled down my cheeks. I sat under a nearby old oak tree to weep.

The yellow water lily spied my sorrow, my longing, and my sadness. Silence embraced me.

I stepped gingerly into my canoe. I paddled my canoe, and I saw beauty. My canoe landed; viewing a trail of deer, I followed the winding path along the lakeshore.

A first home of settlers is revealed—a small one room home, with a food storage shed.

I view evidence of struggle, living on the new land of the USA—a window crack, a chimney in need of repair, no wood cut for a cold winter; roof shingles missing. The delicious red apples had not been picked.

I feel. I touch. I tip-toe. I smell a sweet scent of red wild roses. I stop to pick fresh wild strawberries, enough berries for after-lunch dessert. Filling the palm of my hand, gently holding the berries, I return to my canoe. I know my father will help.

After the church service, guests will be arriving for dinner. Guests will help.

—can you imagine—

A contented grazing cow gave a long moo, encouraging me to move onward. I viewed the pathway.

In the cemetery, I see the gravestone: "Mother." In viewing the gravestone of my mother, her ancient voice speaks. I must remember her voice whispering secrets of nature and kindness of friends.

I listen as meaning is whispered.

The gravestone of "Father" is revealed. I remember my father's quiet voice. I remember his serene humility. I remember his gifts and talent.

A fence line, the rake, the yellow home, the barn, the Christmas tree, I tread onward.

Central Lower Peninsula Michigan

First Settlers—Yellow Home
Allegan
Lower Peninsula, Michigan

Byron Center
Lower Peninsula, Michigan

South Grandville
Lower Peninsula, Michigan

Life Promised

    Early mornings
    Long hours
    Strong back
    Empty pockets

My grandfather and my grandmother, I remember well. I grew taller and matured—my thoughts often led to their pathway—realizing and understanding I needed to remember, to learn from them.
    Tall strong beams of red barns, heralding strength and beauty, were the dreams of the farmer.
    Forever was his thought?
    In the spring, I will plant my crops, and I will watch the tender shoots grow. I will work the fields; I watch my fields, and as I have been promised, the crops will grow.

    I pray.
    I trust.

The rains came; the crops grew—the barns were filled.
Lightning and thunder storms in the dark of night caused the corn and wheat to grow.
On this night, thunder struck loud; lightning bolts broke the sky.
Under my soft red blanket, I cowered.

Promise

    Rain
    Lightning
    Thunder
    Tender Shoots
    Crops
    Maturity
    Beauty
    Blessings

    Hope

Immigrants

Immigrants learned to work with great diligence and trust. Perseverance and determination were the character strengths of my parents and grandparents. We were immigrants.

From early morning to late in the evening, families worked and toiled. With eleven children to feed, clothe, and house, our family was blessed.

Purple flowers of the pathway—the lavender wildflower aster, I loved them all. I see the beauty; I view courage, I view determination—growing in tiny crevices of the heavy red Lake Superior clay. I know the purpose and I view the design. The lavender wild asters gave me strength. Upon the lavender aster, I viewed the yellow bumblebee.

Vibrations of life filled my soul. The hum of the yellow bumblebee quieted my soul and gave me courage. My path led onward.

Immigrants

Church
Guests
Character
Strength

Home
Grandparents
Parents
Children

Pathway
Flowers
Design
Beauty

Courage
Perseverance
Determination
Love

Hope

The Organ—the Piano

I see the organ, and I see the piano standing beneath the open window. The piano lid is open. The piano keys, carved from ivory tusks, are well-used and yellow.

Hesitantly, I touch the edged cracks of the ivory keys. My thoughts, years of practice—then my mind wanders to the tusks of an enormous living elephant—his gentleness.

For years, nimble fingers touched the keys. This piano will tell a story. Two piano keys no longer make a sound. The left soft pedal no longer responds. The elephant weeps.

The barn door opens leading to a pathway; fence posts lead me onward. I smell the hay and straw of summer cuttings.

I view the immigrant home. A home from past;

> Bequeathed in grace
> Rooms of beauty
> Eleven children
> Dinner table welcoming guests

A pathway of blooming flowers; small flowers, intricate flowers, of clover, and grasses grown full in season—I am led quietly onward. I love the smell, a delicate scent of the beauty of creation.

A firefly fly encircles me. Will it land? Will I see it? Yes, I feel it, on my forehead; it has landed.

I sing, as I walk slowly forward in thought. The aroma of the kitchen has drawn me in. My nostrils are permeated with a delicious scent—fragrance of home. I sit and ponder the blessings of my past, of my family, and of my many, many sisters and brothers.

I wonder as I wander.

First Settlers
Allegan, Lower Peninsula, Michigan

Lower Peninsula, Michigan

Shell Barn

Following a new path, I am led to a bright red barn filled with riches of the farmer—a red tractor and hay baler. Heavy wood slabs of a yellow hardwood pine tree are the foundation for this old barn.

The barn was built in 1867.

Freshly painted red, I see the large yellow letters of Shell. Barn doors and windows were strategically placed. In the lower window, a breeze turns the fan. I view a chimney on the roofline; I view the nest of a bald eagle.

Standing below, I watch. I see the eagle. I hear the goslings, and then realize I am the distraction.

I am led by the eagle. As the eagle spread its wings, I move forward, walking under the wings of the eagle.

I find myself skipping in a rhythm with the pace of the Bald Eagle.

I ponder the great beauty.

The Swing Set

A swing set was built by my father; all eleven children would crowd on the swing on Sunday afternoons. We sat on each other's laps.

We sang songs. Our legs moved back and forth, swinging high, soaring with the breeze.

—can you imagine—

Swing Set
Lake Michigan Shoreline
Upper Michigan

Shell Barn US 2
Upper Peninsula, Michigan

Alba, Michigan
Lower Peninsula Michigan

Songs

We sang songs together; we watched the beauty before us. A delightful, almost tamed, flock of spotted seagulls soared above our heads. I remember the colors and I remember the design—black, gray, with white polka dots, and stripes. In awe, I listened to the caw, and watched them swoop encircled within the sparkly, bright blue skies.

Then I heard a bumblebee's buzz; it was the orange-belted bumblebee.

Quietly, the bumblebee sipped the nectar extracting the pollen. I was in awe!

Oh, nature of great beauty! I see you, as I feel your divine presence.

Peek Inside

Once a month, my parents made a long trip to purchase supplies. Basic supplies included: flour, sugar, coffee, wild rice, dried beans, lard, matches, and kerosene. The supply store was located on the southern shores of Upper Peninsula, Lake Michigan. All the supplies were shipped in on long barges from Lower Michigan cities. I spotted the lock; I opened the door, tip-toeing through the large gray door to take a peek. Inside, I viewed the supplies. I was in awe.

Awe

Light	Friendship
Colors	Design
Burden	Strength
Life	Death
Death	Renewal
Flowers	Butterflies
Red Rose	Apples
Warmth	Cold
Renewal	Life
Struggles	Beauty
Songs	Rhythm
Nature	Thought
Supplies	Food
Hope	Wisdom
Door	Opened

Hope

Seagull Flight

Gross Cap Village
Upper Peninsula, Michigan
Supplies

Jamestown
Lower Peninsula, Michigan

Highway 10 Central Lower Peninsula, Michigan

Alba Homestead
Lower Peninsula

First Settlers
Western Upper Peninsula
Michigan

Delicious Red Apples

As light continued to shine, purpose was found within fields of yellow flowers along the pathway of the apple trees. As I walked, I picked a basket of bright delicious red apples. Soon everyone, young and old, began to climb the apple trees to pick the apples and bring in a bounty of delicious red apples.

Applesauce was made, sliced apples were dried, and apples were stored for the winter.

An aroma of fresh-baked apple pies wafted throughout our home and neighborhood. We were blessed. I picked fast, my sisters picked faster, but my brothers picked the fastest.

I loved climbing the apple tree to reach the apples up high. I pulled clumps of five red apples into my basket at one time.

Pond

The nearby pond drew our attention; we were ready to take a swim—with a high jump, off an orange gypsum stone shelf, we found ourselves in the shocking, icy cold spring-fed waters.

The pond, a former gypsum quarry, where water was deep, was behind the home of our pastor.

Our pastor was sympathetic and kind to the children of the Van Ooyen family, realizing we were exhausted and hot, returning from picking the delicious red apples. This was an exceptionally hot summer.

We gave our pastor a basket of apples. Our pastor and his wife were blessed by seven children.

Pewabic Village
Upper Peninsula, Michigan

Blue Dodge Charger—1969

Treasure

A shiny blue Dodge Charger became my father's treasure and a blessing to our family.

Our family of eleven children piled in the blue Dodge Charger. It was Sunday; we were dressed in our Sunday best clothes, and we were on our way to church.

This was a new experience—the new blue Dodge. This car, a Dodge Charger, "is the best," my father said.

Would we fit? Yes. Excitement, joy, chatter, and thankfulness filled our emotions. It was a tight squeeze. The younger children sat on the laps of the older children.

My father drove with pride. I still feel his sense of pride and joy, though I also remember the serious look on his face, His back straightened, as he stared straight ahead, driving between the tree-lined pathways of brightly colored red delicious apple trees.

A careful smile appeared on his face.

Ramsey High School

In the fall, I attended Ramsey High School, built in years 1921-1923 by my forefathers. A cross, the cornerstone, offered thoughts of wisdom and thoughts of love for the children of Ramsey.

The Bible was read; songs were sung and remembered. The verses, having been memorized, were imprinted upon the hearts of all the children.

As I walked the path to Ramsey High School, abruptly, I stopped to listen:

I heard a soft, light voice of a dear elderly friend singing, "Lord Jesus, hear my prayer as I come to you." Finishing her song, Aunt Bertha passed.

Aunt Bertha had been resting on a sitting bench near the Ramsey School entrance.

—take time to imagine—

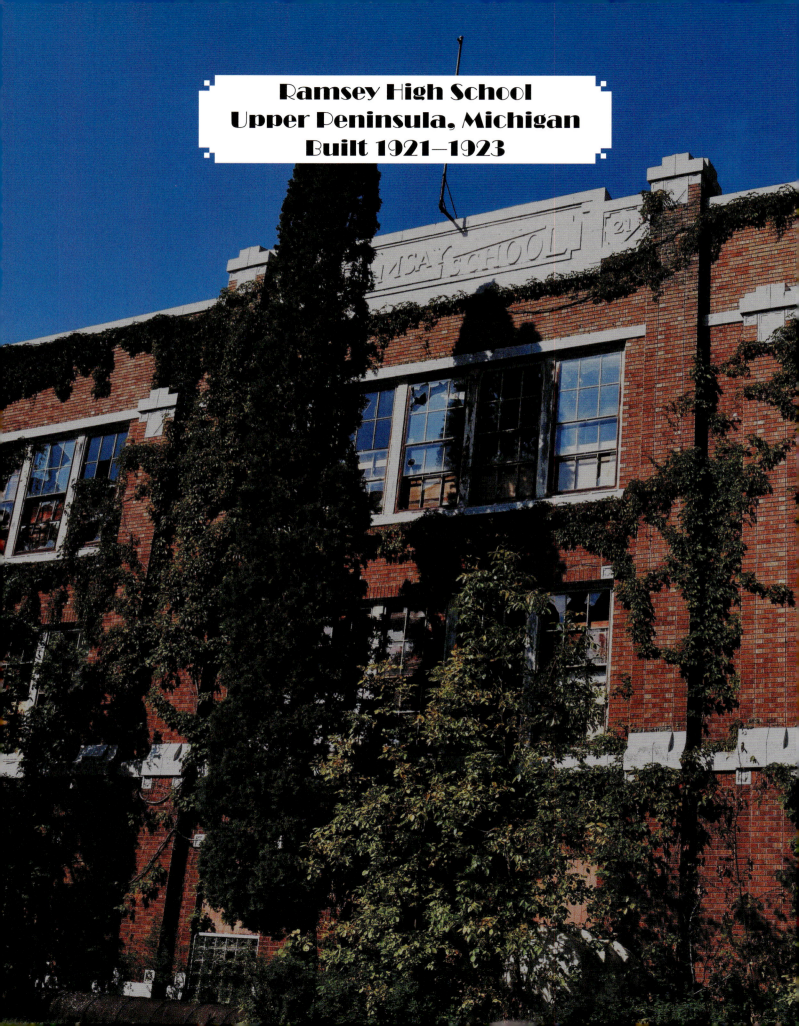

Ramsey High School
Upper Peninsula, Michigan
Built 1921–1923

Ramsey High School—Ramsey Village

Around a bend in the road, I view Ramsey School High School, a large inviting orange brick building—three stories high with a basement, housing classrooms for grades eight through twelve.

The population of Ramsey Village was approximately 1,230 in the early 1900s. With many families having up to six to twelve children, the classrooms were filled.

Ramsey Village was known for iron-ore mining—the fathers and their sons worked the mine. Remnants of the mine are found in the hills behind Ramsey Village.

Ramsey school had teachers for Latin and Speech, offering a solid curriculum for guys and gals. The Ramsey School debate teams became U.P. stars. Sports were number one—with all the students participating. Never will I forget the winning teams; teams of the strongest valiant guys and gals in the U. P. Parents had reason to be proud and they were proud. Their treasured children were happy.

When copper was discovered in the hills, many families moved to Ramsey with hope—hope for a job and an opportunity. The Lutheran church, the Episcopalian church, and the Catholic churches were built. Priests and pastors preached to the families of Ramsey, reminding the fathers and mothers of God's wrath, forgiveness, and of His love.

Fathers gave their children quarters for the offering, explaining to their children, the quarters would provide food and clothing for children less fortunate, in the church and community.

Everyone gave a little; no one went hungry.

Shoes were passed on, coats were passed on, slacks, underwear, and boots; all were passed on. Churches made certain everyone had a warm coat for the cold winter. I received boots with holes in the heels—putting my feet in a bread bag, kept my feet dry.

My feet were always cold.

Everyone had just enough. In the evenings we were warmed by the fireplace, singing songs as we watched the flames of a hot fire. Apple tree firewood, burning hot and slowly, kept our homes warm, even in minus twenty degrees.

Ramsey High School Students

Ramsey School grew; teachers were hired, becoming forever beloved teachers. Sports drew the families together. Loudly, the parents cheered, with Ramsey High School students becoming winners.

Excitement was perpetually in the air. The Village of Ramsey prospered.

Children learned to read and to write; evenings were filled with practicing arithmetic, memorizing the figures and numbers. Arithmetic speed tests and spelling tests occurred weekly.

Huck Finn, Tom Sawyer, The Diary of Anne Frank were required reading.

The Bible was read first in the early morning, and the school day ended with prayer.

Classrooms were filled.

Daily, our fathers and mothers prayed for wisdom.

Soon my cousins arrived to join us. Together, we walked the paths of the fields and played find-me, catch-me in the cornfields. The corn leaves were a dark green color with stalks so high our heads could not be seen. The corn was light yellow, super sweet, and scrumptious.

I skipped and jumped joyfully when I walked to school. I was so happy.

Spring Water

Salt waters were found in many wells of Upper Peninsula of Michigan, but in Ramsey, spring water flowed from beneath a railway bridge; the water was sweet.

Neighbors came from afar to fill water jugs and basins.

I still hear the gentle rushing of the fresh water gurgling out from beneath the railroad bridge. I relished the fresh, cool, sweet water as the water rushed over my toes. I sipped refreshing water from the palm of my hand.

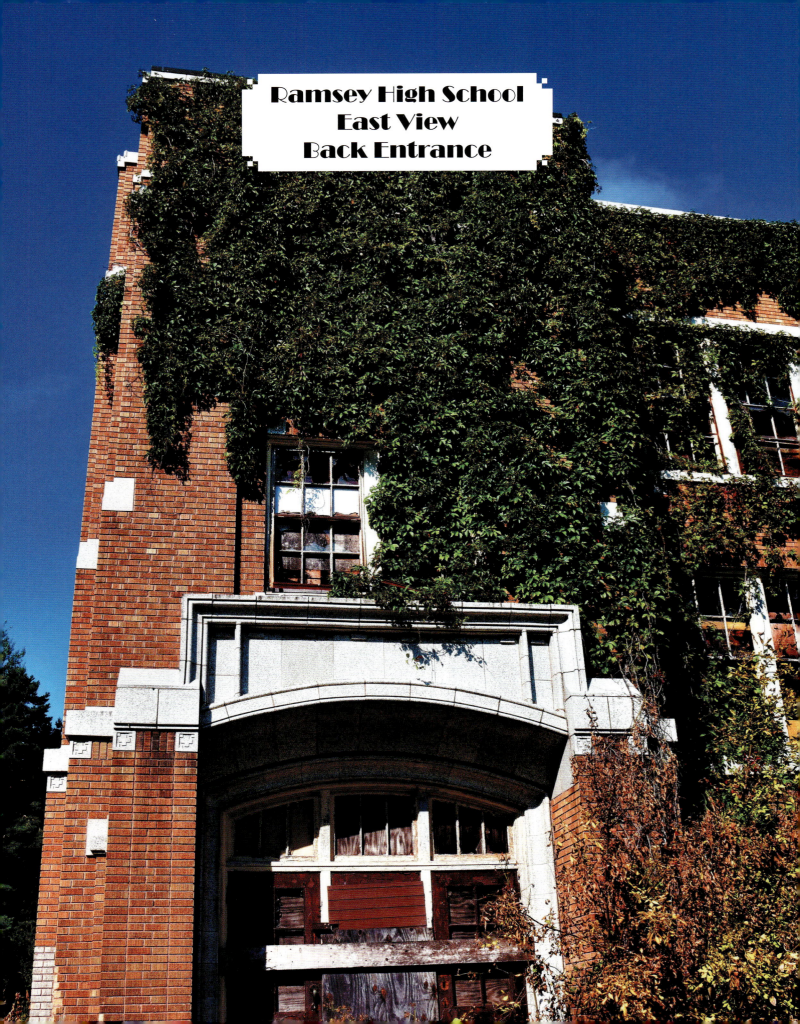

Cornerstone Cross 1921–1923

Sweet Cool
Spring Water

Home—Hope—Cousins
Highway 117

Family

Our family lived in a large home off Highway 117; the spring water was sweet. Everyone was welcome.

When my cousins arrived, a camp was set up in the backyard of our home. A life of "utopia," as my father would say. An organ and a piano filled the back room of our home; white lacy curtains waved through the windows, as warm summer breezes filled our home. I saw light, warm sunbeams shining with dazzle from one window through to another. Our home was filled with happiness.

Our cousins joined our family in our evening Bible reading. I heard voices singing. We sang with loud, strong voices, in gusto style, always in tune. I heard my mom encouraging us, "louder, louder."

It was good. We shared our water and our food. Crops were planted and vegetables grew in the dark rich loam earth. We knew our camping guests and cousins could hear our singing—possibly the words were heard and understood.

Hope

Sharing
Welcome

An Organ
A Piano

Sunbeams
Happiness

Light
Happiness

Singing
Neighbors

Light

The Fire

We ate together, and rejoiced with many blessings. Children of all ages played games as we sat on the soft red blanket on Sunday afternoons. It was summertime; I felt the warm breeze.

"Help, the house is on fire!" I heard my cousin scream. The kitchen stove had caught fire. All the children were in panic. We lost our house to the fire, our home. Our parents lost hope. We lost everything; our cousins left. Tears were shed. We wept; we all lost hope. Could we ever find hope again?

I remember the long clothesline—with clothes flapping in the soft, fragrant breezes, drying in the warm rays of the sun. Sheer, soft lace curtains hanging in the windows were now singed and torn. I stared in unbelief at the cracked, fire-blackened glass.

I see it all, my memories are vivid. Even the window frames were in flames. Our hearts were saddened. I felt the heat of the fire. I was afraid. I ran, and ran, to escape. I stumbled on a briar. I was fearful. I lay in long grasses, amidst briars. I wept in fear.

Our house for many years was now uninhabitable. I returned to join our family of eleven children. Everyone, all the children, were safe.

We had no home insurance—insurance was never thought of. Our dreams were impacted with fright. We stood in a circle, holding hands. We watched our house burn, as tears rolled down our cheeks—younger siblings were openly sobbing.

Though the future we did not know, the organ remained waiting for another stanza. The piano also remained, leaning against the wall of the spacious family room, waiting for the touch of my father's fingers. Every Sunday evening, my mom would make a special Sunday evening brunch while listening to her children sing. Our mom would view her children singing through the kitchen window—now what would be our future? Where would we find hope?

From the light of the earth sprang hope. Upon my new pathway I watched the opening of a flower bud—a flower of hope. The wild soft pink pitcher plants were in full bloom along the lakeshore, with flower heads turned toward the sun; I found hope.

I wept, while I silently walked. I pondered, but was renewed as again; light brought hope. I see, I touch, and I smell, realizing I had found renewed hope.

I rejoiced. A flower was blooming.

Camp Tent City

Piano

**Organ
Remains Behind**

**Facing Sunshine
Pitcher Plant flower**

Flowers of Hope

Porch Vines

My Gold-Ribbon-Star, Prized, Black-and-White Holstein Cow Watches

The wagon was loaded with supplies; a red bush of all fall colors decorated the supply wagon.

Filled with winter supplies of flour, sugar, coffee, and kerosene, we understood the expectation for the Upper Michigan winter snows. Brisk winds blew with fierce certainty.

Beside the loaded wagon stood my gold-ribbon, star Holstein—her dark eyes followed me. I felt her warm breath.

Tales are told of the winter of 1938—an icy cold winter; snow drifts measured to be twenty-five feet deep. Fathers became lost; mothers fed the chickens, and became disoriented. It seemed the winds would never cease. Many frozen chickens were found in the springtime—frozen chicken eggs were found in their nests.

This was a winter to be forever remembered.

I shudder, the purpose I ponder, and I renew my thoughts.

—if one could only imagine—

Black Stallion Horse

Northwest Ironwood

Due to extreme cold winters, struggles were constant for immigrants. Winds blew fiercely. Many water wells tasted of salt; gardens did not bear fruit or grains. The farmer became ill, and his children went to bed hungry. The farmer and his wife grieved. It was a time of great sadness—daily, the farmer carried his burdens on his back.

Fresh Water

He leads, I ponder, and I am silent. Fresh waters were found under the railroad gateway.

The stallion horse quenched his thirst.

Immigrants shared the fresh water and spread words of hope. Once again light was shining upon the immigrant families. The families shared their grains and their fresh water.

Delicious Red Apples

Apples grew everywhere. Many years ago, the first immigrants from Finland brought apple trees to Upper Peninsula of Michigan. Years later, Johnny Appleseed spread delicious red apple tree seeds upon the rich soil of Upper Peninsula Michigan land, with great anticipation. Apples supplied needed wealth to the farmers of the land.

Along roadsides, apple trees are found everywhere.

Apples evolved into hope.

Churches were built, and faith was reborn. Schools enjoyed many new students; the community grew, schools grew in number.

Hope was restored. Hope became light.

Great Sadness

In early springtime, new immigrants arrived in northwestern Ironwood. I felt the struggle, I saw the struggle as the fields were plowed, and the harvest was brought in; delicious red apple trees were planted. But the father did not have strength, and the mother was critically ill.

Their precious beautiful boy child passed in childbirth. I trembled and shuddered for the family. Their water was salty.

I tasted salty tears on my cheek.

The pastor of my church made a visit to bring a hot meal to our neighbors, along with plenty of hot coffee. My mother stopped by to bring an apple pie. My father plowed the fields. The neighbors brought in the harvest.

The church prayed; a collection was taken. The family received the collection—all of it.

The apple trees gave fruit, and the father shared the delicious red apples with the members of the church. Great rejoicing and thankfulness, as life became a celebration of hope.

Pink pitcher plant flowers gave me a nod.

Purpose

Struggle
Passing
Tears

Caring
Hope
Light

New Immigrant
Church
Celebration

Hope

Supply Wagon

Spring

Springtime arrived. The robins and cardinals flew back. The hummingbirds fluttered their wings as nectar was sipped, and pollen was stored. I viewed the honeybees' hind legs laden with pollen. This tasty liquid would supply new life next spring.

The location of my new school was in Northern Lower Peninsula. My parents made a move to the warmer climate of the Lower Peninsula of Michigan. I was excited to attend a new two-room school built with wisdom of the forefathers.

I remember the staircase that led to the school library. I remember the windows—many windows, through which light would shine.

I loved to look through the windows and follow the rays of the sun shining upon the deep green leaves of corn.

I imagined myself walking along a long row of corn. I got lost.

Today is my birthday; I am thirteen years old.

I am so excited! In our family, age thirteen meant adulthood; live with responsibility and be trusted. I spoke of my mom, as my mother.

My view through the window pane of our new house carried me into fields of flowers, and yellow bumblebees. Light of sun rays gave me hope, as I gazed across the open fields, thickened by a clover crop of red clover.

Shining beams of light encompassed my view. Rainbows of light glistened upon the dew of the small flowers of red clover.

I was thrilled to be in a new house and a new school.

I straightened my back, and walked forward with hope.

Fern School Dist. No. 3 CW.1906

Bringing in Hay

Bessemer
Upper Peninsula, Michigan

Lake City
Lower Peninsula, Michigan

First Settlers, Western Upper Peninsula, Michigan

Highway 20 First Settlers
Lower Peninsula, Michigan

Ironwood Episcopalian Church

Churches were built; church pews were filled. Following the church service, guests would join our family for Sunday dinner. Our family was blessed having left the freezing winters of the Upper Peninsula.

My father helped to build the church. Once again, he enjoyed playing the church organ on Saturday evenings and Sunday mornings. When my father passed, my father's home organ was donated to St. John Lutheran church. To this day, the organ remains in the church, and continues to be played. My mother's book sales support repairs of the organ at St. John's Church. My father's photograph has been permanently placed on a corner of the organ; memories of my father will forever remain.

On Sunday afternoon, in a blizzard, father and I were privileged to perform a flute-and-organ recital in the Ironwood Episcopalian Church—a recital for the church and the community. A blizzard raged outside, yet the audience arrived. A reception of cookies and cakes, tenderly baked, was ready for the recital audience and the performers.

"Jesu, Joy of Man's Desiring," a favorite sacred selection, composed by Johann Sebastian Bach, was etched in the souls of all in attendance.

Jesu, Joy of Man's Desiring
Johann Sebastian Bach

Jesu, joy of man's desiring
Holy wisdom, love most bright;
Drawn by Thee, our souls aspiring,
Soar to uncreated light.

Word of God, our flesh that fashioned.
With the fire of life impassioned.
Striving still to truth unknown,
Soaring, dying round Thy throne.

Through the way where hope is guiding,
Hark, what peaceful music rings?
Where the flock, in Thee confiding,
Drink of joy from deathless springs.

Theirs is beauty's fairest pleasure;
Theirs is wisdom's holiest treasure.
Thou dost ever lead Thine own,
In the love of Joys unknown.

Covington Catholic Church
Upper Peninsula, Michigan

The Lake

A most favorite time for me was swimming with my father. I love to swim. My father loved to swim.

On a travel to a lake with my family, we passed gigantic round bales of straw. I loved to climb the large bales, as a fresh warm aroma of yellow straw filled my nostrils.

For certain, the farmer was blessed by this good summer. This was a summer when a dessert of apple cake, was served at all our meals. Delicious red apples continued to provide blessings.

At our lake, we would swing on leather-covered swings, and from the swings we would jump into the icy cold, spring-fed waters; swinging and jumping, upward as high as our small bodies would travel in the warm air breezes. Splash!

What great memories of my father. His straight, jet-black hair almost fully covered his dark brown eyes. My father was handsome. I will never forget! My father was always kind.

I loved him so much.

—if you could only imagine—

Swing Set Leather Seats

—Imagine—

Eden Dist. No 2. 1892
Eastern Upper Michigan, Lower Peninsula

First Settlers
Western Upper Peninsula

First Settlers
Highway 117, Upper Peninsula, Michigan

Highway 20
Lower Peninsula, Michigan

Van Ooyen Family

Van Ooyen Family—Father (standing), Mother, children, with dog, Julie.
Carrier-Table—Chevy Impala Station Wagon

Wasp Hive

I Look Upward

Hanging from a lower branch, I view perfection within the unique design of a wasp hive. Standing quietly, I stare into the wasp nest. A wasp is retreating from the hive.

The apples are ripe. Bright delicious red apples, an Upper Peninsula treasure.

Wheels continue to turn. Cows moo.

Family Camping

On the edge of the woods, treading lightly, I stumbled upon remnants of my father's skill: Is this a picnic table or a car top carrier?

I remember our car top carrier, when it was filled with children's clothes, food, and treasures needed for camping. I remember the hidden campsite deep in the woods, and off to the right, I see a picnic table for eleven children.

Yes, I remember, it was a car top carrier and also a picnic table. To lessen the weight, my father drilled holes along the lengthwise center of each plank of wood. Ingenious was my father.

The carrier-table was filled and ready for the camping trip, accompanying the family on many family tenting vacation trips.

Vacations were always filled with wonder and mystery.

A large blue racer snake, a wolf spider, a striped white-and-black skunk, a long-twilled porcupine, a beaver with a long tail slap, white-tailed deer, a raccoon, loud buzzing horse flies, swarms of mosquitoes, ground bees pulling a spider into its run, an old lengthy garter snake—its skin left behind for me, and stunning green-laced dragon flies—I loved them all.

I viewed the amazing colors and great design. I skipped with joy!

Carrier Table Bench

Uncovering the Picnic Table

Garter Snake

Snake Skin

Family Motto Ceramic Bowl by sister, Ellie

Table for Eleven plus Two

In full view, I see the picnic table for eleven children—rough-hewn oak wood, not maple and not pine, but oak—strength for the family of eleven children.

I will remember forever the words attached to the back of the car top carrier, artistically carved into an octagonal sign, by my father.

"Work, Share, Fun" with "God" engraved in the center.

The piano traveled with the family to a larger house—home for the eleven. We were a dangly, gangly, tired gang of children, traveling impatiently, and cramped into the blue Dodge Charger. Manners were always expected with an accompanied smile. Hard and diligent work was always the expectation.

In the afternoons, we made s'mores. In our large backyard, my father had built a tall, gigantic fireplace of bright red bricks. So high was the chimney, I could not see over it. I had to tip my head backward until the back of my head touched my shoulder to see the top red stone, Lake Superior, clay bricks.

The fire coals were perfect. We fried the many fish our mother caught. The fish were made into fish patties—never knowing what was hidden in the patty—our thoughts were that fish bones had been ground up and added into the patties.

We ate s'mores to "top it off," as our mother would say, toasty and crispy—scrumptious and delicious. We leaned the long, homemade pointed sticks on a thirteen-inch circumference stump, ready for our next wood fire. The large frying pan was set aside for another fish fry day.

The sticks were perfectly whittled and shaped. All eleven children whittled their own roasting sticks.

We shared our father's sharp knife when whittling the pointed sticks.

—take time to imagine—

Golden Glow Restaurant

Fireplace Cinders

Family Picnic Table

Fire Pit

Our eyes would peer into the fire to find the best coals; teasingly, we bickered over a best spot, as marshmallows melted and burst into flame. Our fingers were sticky and sweet—we licked our fingers.

On my right hand, the second two fingers touched the coals. Ouch! My sister also accidently placed a stick, with a burning marshmallow, on the cheek of her face. Ouch!

The pain lasted many weeks.

Stinging burns are never forgotten.

Ontonagon

For a special trip, summertime of 1949, we camped at a park in Ontonagon.

We were privileged to visit a homestead built in 1854 for the indigenous people of the Ontonagon area—a farm built with purpose. Tasks were assigned to residents: daily chores, gardening and farming, milking cows, cleaning and preparing meals, as well as caring for residents in the home.

Finest Holstein cows were raised on this homestead. "Eat Light with Beef " is signage on the southeast outside wall. This home is now spoken of as the "Poor House." The "Soup Bone Lumberjacks" were given comfort and food.

The second floor was built to store water for the men's and women's washrooms. Before the days of Social Security, this was how the community cared for the poor. I feel the tenderness. I view the beauty.

Our family brought cookies for all; we were invited in for tea.

Inside, I viewed the walls. The walls were papered in green and pink, colors of fresh lime-green grass and leaves, among many soft pink flowers. My eyes followed the green vines on the walls, as the vines wound up toward the ceiling. I counted the leaves and watched the flowers. Growing as I watched, I am certain.

I will never forget the privilege to view and understand the loving care for the less fortunate living on the Ontonagon Poor Farm Homestead.

Ontonagon Poor Farm Homestead South Front View

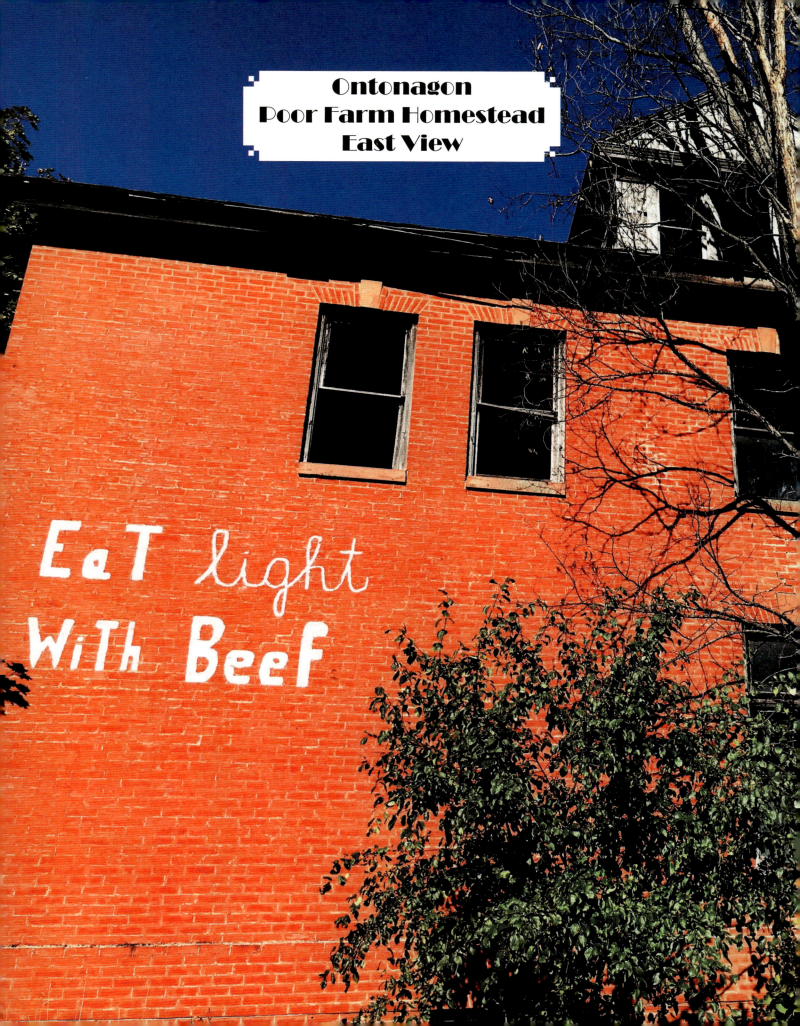

Red Truck

Ontonagon—Poor Farm Homestead

Imagine our family of eleven children being given permission to explore the grounds behind the Ontonagon Poor Farm Homestead.

We did.

I heard a horse neighing, and then found five sleek black horses in a large barn, with one large stallion in the pasture. This horse was the only male. We were warned not to go near him. I watched him, viewing the horse's majestic beauty. The shine of his dark black coat caught my eyes; I yearned to ride him. I stared into his dark black eyes as the stallion stared back at me. What were his thoughts, I pondered.

The stallion gave a snort.

My shoes were covered in mud and horse manure.

Across the pond, behind the homestead, I heard many loud moos coming from the direction of another large barn. A herd of fifty-five Holstein cows were eating grain, and being readied for milking.

Enough hands were "on deck" to help with the milking. Our family helped to milk the cows. We milked with our hands—a first for me. Bending over, close to the udders, I milked a cow.

I was offered a glass of fresh milk and a taste of cheese.

Milk and cheese had become a significant source of income to keep the Poor House Homestead self-supporting for many years.

In the back, on the right side of the homestead was a pond. We went swimming with my father. The spring-fed waters were icy cold. We climbed on my father's shoulders and dove into the deep cold water.

To warm up, we went for a walk with my father on a trail that had footprints of white-tailed deer and a raccoon. The young fawn prints were our pathway, among the early spring flowers of the wild apple trees.

The apple trees were in full bloom, covered with white and pink blossoms. We picked a few branches, bringing a beautiful large bouquet of apple tree blossoms to our mother. Our mother was delighted. Today was our mother's birthday, May 10; she was thirty-nine years old. We loved our mother.

—can you imagine—

Apple Tree Blossoms
—imagine—

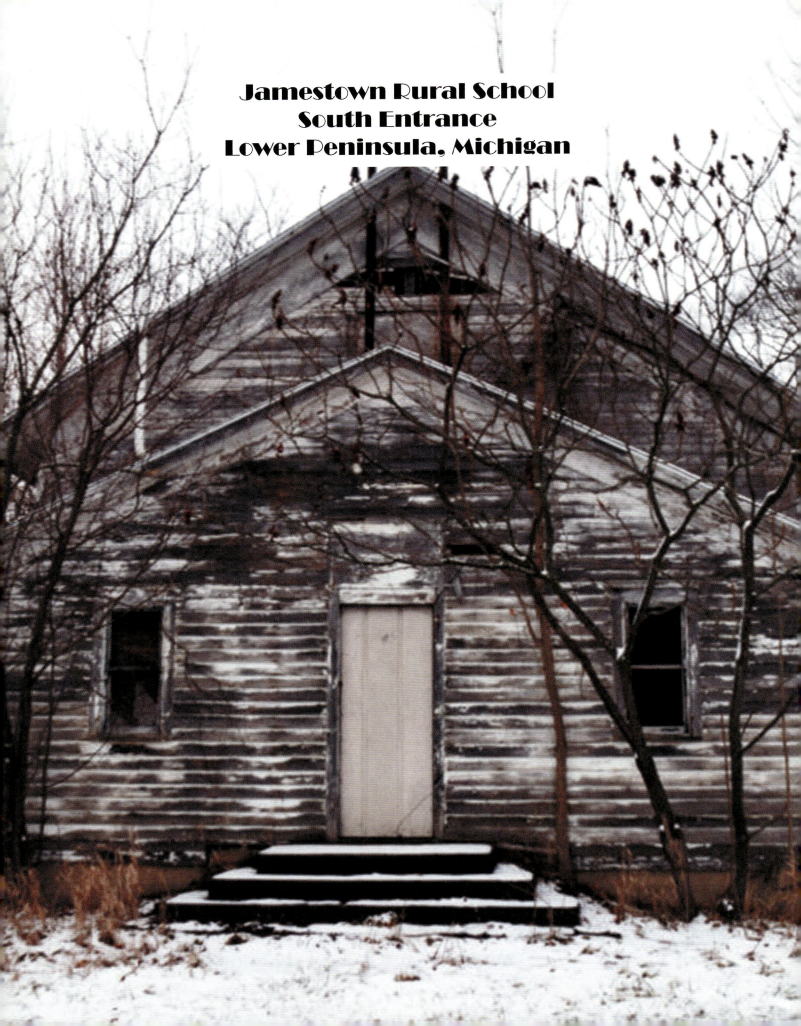

Jamestown Schoolhouse
West Side

Chimney

Window Vines

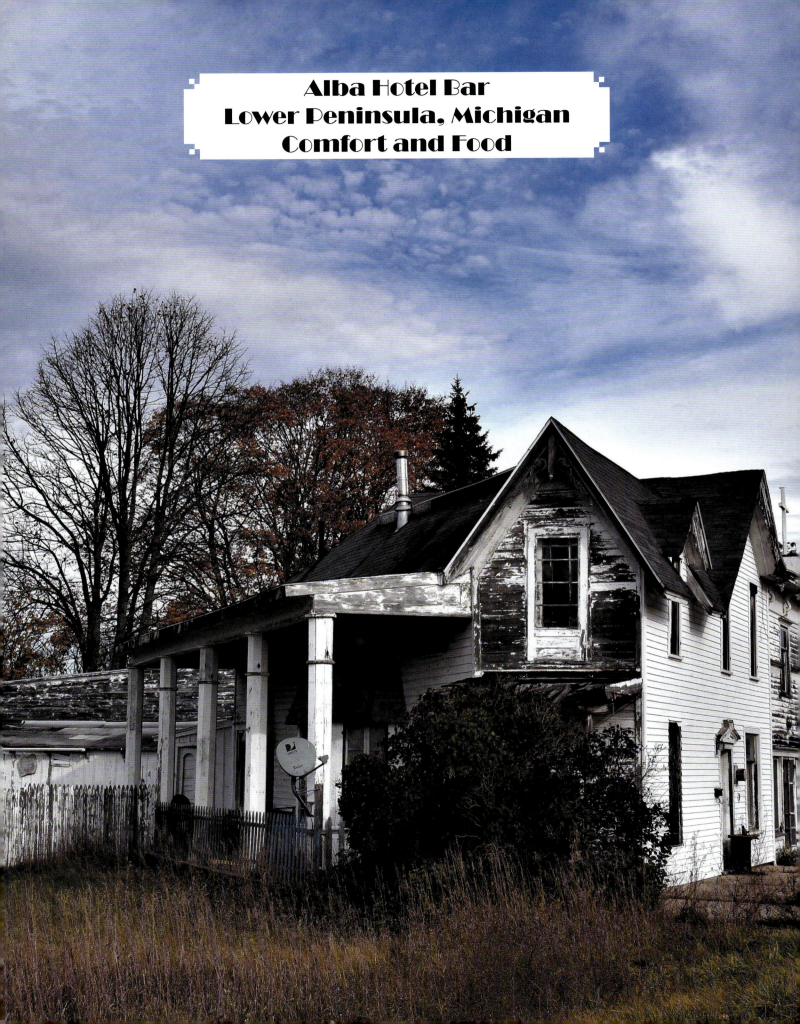

Rejoicing

Our family rejoiced with our father and mother in the blessings of another year.

Our determined, furiously independent mother of great strength always kept her children in line, organizing the chores of cleaning our home: polishing silver, dusting furniture, cleaning windows, and washing loads of dishes—yes, the children were the dishwashers.

The floor had to be swept, mopped, polished, and shined every week on Saturday morning. We took turns doing the dusting, and we all helped with care of the younger children—feeding, bathing, dressing, and changing diapers.

Chores were expected. All the children were assigned chores.

My father made a list, to help us take turns amiably.

I chuckle. A list was posted weekly on the window ledge by the kitchen sink. Our names were on it; two rows of names listed in rotation, beginning with the day of the week. To be the dishwasher, or the dish dryer, the list answered the question for the day of the week.

Doing chores without complaint was the expectation. This was the way it was.

We had no reason to quarrel.

Dagh	**Naam**	
Maandag	Kathy	Anne
Dinsdag	Jane	Peter
Woensdag	Judy	Ellie
Donderdag	Amy	Cal
Vrijdag	John	Al
Zaterdag	Troy	Kathy
Zondag	Anne	Jane

if only you could imagine—

Pathway

Walking in the early morning, I followed the pathway of a fawn; I viewed and admired a low wood flowering bush, the winterberry red berry. The forest wood-floor was covered with the red berries and shiny green leaves of Winterberry flowers. On the edge of the woods, bears walked, enjoying and engorging on the Winterberries.

I found bear skeet nearby—a large seedy pile. I walked in silence.

I was in thought, as I knew I had to be careful. I should not snap a branch.

High above, I heard the call of the whippoorwill—a call of warning. Stepping on soft pine needles below a large yellow pine tree, I continued on my pathway in silence. The mama bear and her two cubs would not spot me, though I did spot them, as they scuttled noiselessly up a nearby tall oak tree.

For a long time, I watched the young cubs, clinging to the highest tree branch, with the mother bear below. The cubs were looking down watching me. I smiled.

Ahead, and slightly to my right, I spotted a garden snake, silently slithering beneath a log. The skin was left for me, a gift. The snake moved into hiding, while three young snakes came crawling out from beneath the log.

The following summer, I found a snake between the mattresses of my cabin bed. I was not afraid, but my visitors were. Up on a nearby chair they jumped. I heard a piercing scream. This garter snake was five feet in length, with a one-inch circumference.

I stood still in thought, would this be the same snake I spotted beneath the log last summer?

—can you imagine—

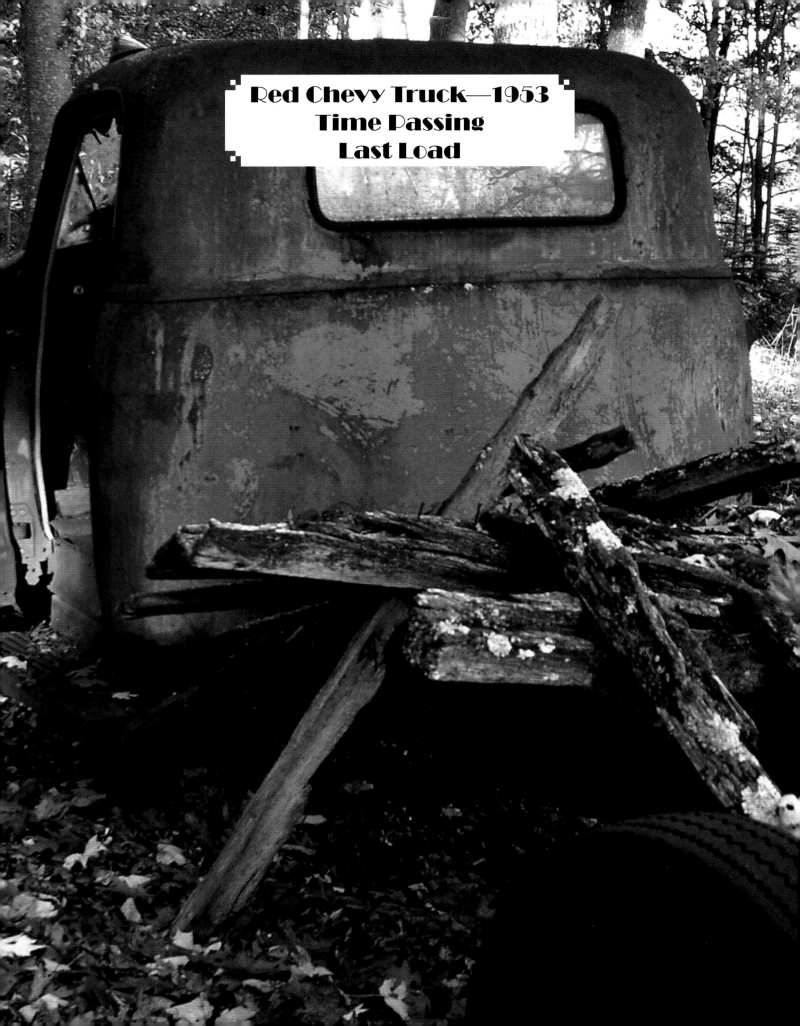

Red Chevy Truck—1953
Time Passing
Last Load

Red Truck
Time Past

Walking along the edge of the woods, peering through dense trees, I spotted an old red Truck, hidden within a strand of trees with a load of cut wood ready for stacking. My father treasured his large red Chevy 1953 truck. Was this my grandfather's red truck?

Time has passed.

My father drove his red truck every day to pick up wood for our old-fashioned, wrought iron, wood-heating stove. My father also brought many loads of wood to the neighbors. On his drive, a neighbor, who had lost his leg in a logging accident, received five cords of wood from my father. My father neatly stacked the wood beside the back door in order that his neighbor's elderly dear wife could bring the wood indoors.

In the winter it took twenty-plus cords of wood to keep a house warm. "Stupid work," my father remarked, but he cut the wood, determined his home would be cozy warm.

My father used his hands and fingers to play the organ of the church, and his bright mind to read great books, specifically the study of music of Johann Sebastian Bach. I would often find my father reading deep religious writings—his thoughts always of great depth.

Covington Catholic Church

Every Sunday our family attended church in the morning and evening, with lunch planned at noontime for family and visitors. Sunday was a day of church, or as was said, "Day of rest." I was not fond of this kind of rest; I hoped to run on a path of discovery deep in the woods.

Our church in the village of Covington was a beautiful white, well-kept church. I loved the tall steeple. The church had an organ and my father was the organist. My father's weekends were kept busy planning services and playing the organ; two services on Saturday evening, and three services on Sunday morning.

All of the locals, the entire community, attended church.

On my pathway, lay a white feather. I felt divine presence. "Lead me on," I sang.

Highway 28
Upper Peninsula, Michigan

Highway 117

Covington Catholic Church

My Eye on You

Yellow Home

My uncles, aunts, and many cousins lived in small homes painted in bright colors. I loved the yellow home of my Tante ("aunt") Janny. Barns were built large, constructed from strong beams of yellow hardwood pine.

My Tante Janny was fit and cheery. Memories of Tante Janny are rooted in her loving creative, artistic talent, and kind demeanor.

Tante Janny adored children. She also baked the best apple-rhubarb pie. We often spent time at her home playing games; guaranteed to be followed by a large slice of apple-rhubarb pie.

I licked off the whipped cream first.

We ran through her fields of wildflowers; dashing through white daisies, and yellow black-eyed Susan flowers.

My favorite flower is the allium flower. Peering upon a pink flower head, I witnessed a large yellow bumble bee gathering pollen. This delicate pink flower is of the onion flower family; tasty in summertime hot dishes.

Large yellow bumblebees are found throughout the Upper Peninsula of Michigan; bumblebees are Upper Peninsula pollinators.

In understanding life in the U.P., I knew life was dependent on pollinators; though once I witnessed a young boy stepping on a bumblebee. I would never consider stepping on a yellow bumblebee.

I loved the yellow soft fur and lacy black wings, a stripped contrasting color of beauty and design.

—can you imagine—

First Settlers

St. John's Lutheran Church

Lake Superior—Indian Maiden

Best friends lived on the shores of Lake Superior, where one could easily find a favorite sandy spot on the beach for a picnic. Summertime Sunday afternoon church services were held at Little Girls Point.

Little Girls Point remains the land of Native American Indians of Upper Peninsula Michigan—treasured lands with fresh springs of water, shallow streams, and freshwater lakes.

Lush clear creeks meander through the woodlands, filled with eight-inch, colorful, brightly speckled trout. Native American Indians hunted, fished and lived understanding nature and the treasures nature offers.

Joy, thanksgiving, and peace encircled the Native American camps until, one afternoon; a young Indian maiden swam out into the icy Lake Superior waters. The waves were strong and dangerous, the winds blew, and in unbelief, the waters took the young Maiden out farther and farther. The young Indian maiden never returned.

To this day the memory remains. This historical event is forever a heart-rending story of the young Indian maiden. A permanent sign has been placed in the county park of Little Girls Point.

In reverence, I walk, and I marvel in fear of the waves. "I Wonder as I Wander." Feeling tears trickling down my cheeks, in silence, I walk and I ponder. I am overwhelmed with sorrow, as I feel the pain of great loss.

Indian Maiden

Beach
Water
Waves
Wind

Tears
Sorrow
Pain
Loss

The waves
The Storm
Forever
Indian Maiden

Hope

Indian Maiden

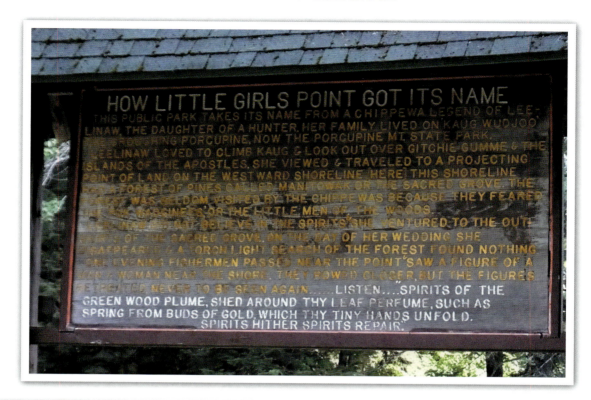

Oman's Blue House Agate Rock Shop

Little Girls Point

Little Girls Point
Well-House
Seagulls

Home of the Pastor

Garage

Our Pastor

Our pastor was a country pastor. He was kind and wise. His home was built on a large tract of land. He had many cows, and horses, along with seventeen chickens, and one rooster.

His chickens laid many eggs—enough to share eggs with members of his church.

His congregants helped with chores of milking the cows and bringing in the hay. They adored him. The pastor and his beautiful wife had thirteen children.

While milking the cows and riding his horses, my pastor gave thoughts to the next Sunday sermon. The Sunday sermons topics were always centered on farming and his many unique experiences with the animals.

I loved going to church. One time, the sermon theme was about a raccoon stealing eggs from his chickens and hiding them (would the raccoon find his eggs?—my thought).

How was this sermon theme applied to the lives of his congregants?

The raccoon was my pet and followed me wherever and whenever I walked. I raised and trained him. The raccoon had just been born when I found him. I fed him milk using a very tiny toy baby bottle.

I named him Racky.

Surprises were always in store for our pastor, a lover of animals and nature.

My aunts, uncles, and cousins continued building homes and barns in the vicinity of the church. Many barns were of unique design, to house the many animals. My uncle's pigs, horses, and cows grew in number. His farm became large, covering many acres.

The milk, with rich cream on top, was scrumptious; the cheese was delicious, and the eggs were large only. I loved the eggs that had two yokes. Geese and ducks were added to the farm, and their eggs were even larger. The large eggs were always a delicious treat.

—if you could only imagine—

The Water Was Sweet

The Pastor of Trinity Lutheran Church had a home with a garage—the garage being a very special gift from Trinity Lutheran Church. Our Pastor was loved, as my father was loved.

As I silently walked in the fields behind the home of my pastor, I was struck by wondrous, dazzling, beauty—being encircled by tiny insects of many colors. Green-laced flies, dark brown and green crickets, monarch butterflies, slate-blue butterflies, green and white cabbage moths, the mysterious firefly—all insects of the fields. I was endeared to all the insects.

I know them all by name.

Spider webs paved my pathway, as dew sparkled on the webbing design. A "miracle of all miracles," my father's words, as insects became trapped in the spider's web, and then became food for the spider.

I watched. I was amazed.

Within the large barn of my pastor, I heard the long, deep moos of a large herd of Holstein cows. I smelled the beckoning warm breath. Their curious eyes caught mine.

One last time, I peered through the light shining through cracks of the panes of the window.

Beautiful memories of my pastor filled my spirit and my mind. My pastor's family immigrated two generations before my parents. Our pastor was a cousin of my parents.

The deep well water was sweet.

Highway 10
Lower Peninsula, Michigan

Bessemer Courthouse

My footprint was imprinted upon the red clay bricks, as I traveled to the courthouse, built of the ancient red clay brick stones. Red clay was found among the red clay cliffs on Lake Superior shores. I was mesmerized, remembering bathing in soft red clay on the Lake Superior shoreline of Little Girls Point County Park.

The red clay bricks will last forever—bricks future generations will treasure in perpetuity.

Within the walls of the courthouse, the registered deeds are found. These priceless treasures are entombed in the basement vaults of the redbrick building, the courthouse of Bessemer, Michigan.

Legal questions were asked; legal questions were answered, all in a friendly Upper Peninsula of Michigan manner—most often with a great respect for the Upper Peninsula Community of Bessemer.

My parents are Yoopers; I became a Yooper. With great community respect, the recording of my parent's death, are found within the walls of Bessemer Courthouse. Their love for all things beautiful in nature, and community, lives on forever.

I admired and respected the Yooper's. Yooper, a name proudly given to the immigrants of the U.P., are mostly of the Finnish and Swedish descent.

Copper Mines

In the copper mines of Upper Michigan, bright orange copper was found to be the highest quality copper in the entire world. From the ore mined in the miles-deep tunnels and shafts, copper was extracted; pure copper runs were discovered. Worldwide sales provided riches to the immigrants of the Upper Peninsula of Michigan.

Churches were built, schools grew in size, and families were large—several families having fifteen children. The fathers and sons worked the mines. The mothers and daughters prepared the food. Family life was fulfilled and happy.

Trusting life would be forever happy was the thought.

—can you imagine—

Bessemer Courthouse

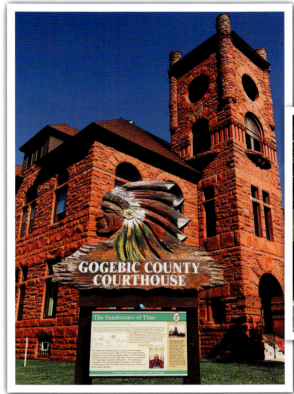

Presque Isle, Wisconsin

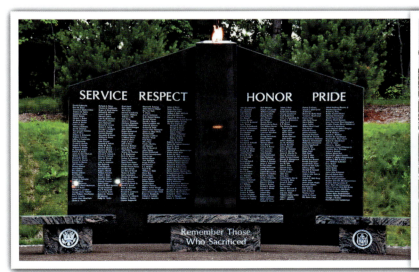

Service Respect Honor Pride

Tunnel Collapse—1926

Finely tuned, uniquely engineered heavy equipment was positioned for deep mining, in hope for a copper run. Machinery was shipped to the Upper Peninsula, from Finland and Sweden.

Deep underground tunnels were cored into the earth; men traveled into the dark tunnels with lights on their helmets and a lunch pail in hand. With absolute determination, with trust, with endurance, with perseverance—the men with their sons, every day in the early morning, traveled into the dark, deep shafts.

Courageous and strong, they were, until a loud rumble echoed through the tunnels. A piercing scream was audible; the men trembled, realizing the rumble was a tunnel collapse.

Fifty-one men and boys were lost—all fathers and sons of the community. Forty-two women lost their husbands; 132 children lost their fathers, on November 3, 1926. Many bodies were left entombed. The day is commemorated in most villages of the Upper Peninsula—loss and devastation of the tunnel collapse will never be forgotten.

Tears were shed throughout all of Upper Peninsula, Michigan.

The women were overcome, but the women grew strong and fearsome. Yet, as if in battle, the women would not be overcome. Their children became strong. To endurance they pledged forever. To this day the women and children carry on with undeniable strength.

My thoughts bend to great respect.

—if one could only imagine—

Cliff Copper Mine

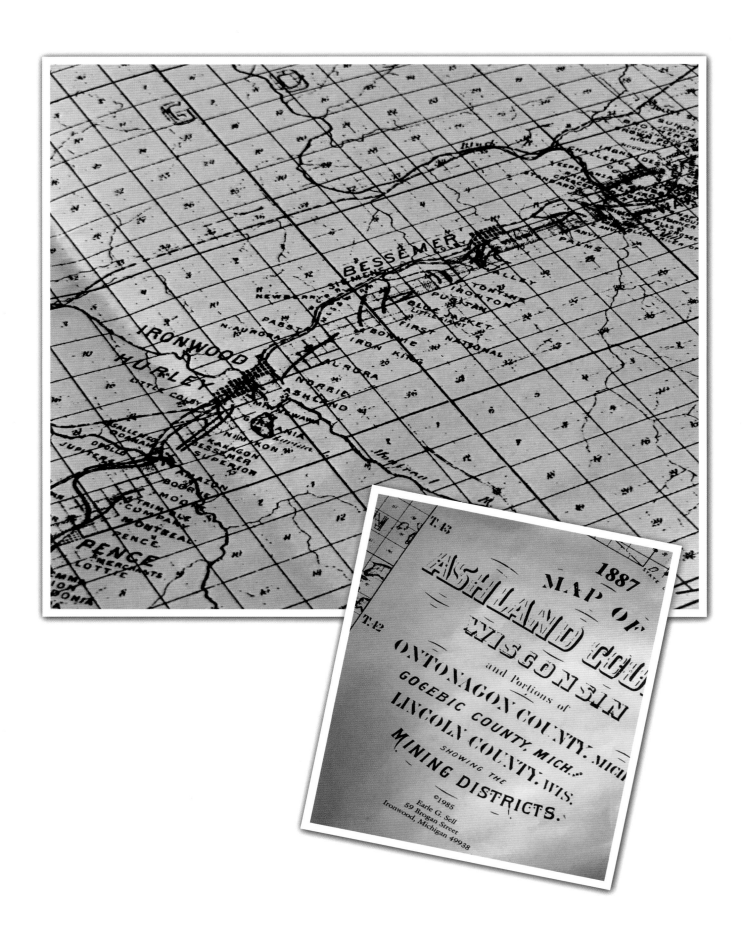

Hoekstra-Van Ooyen Cabin

At this moment, my thoughts move to my cabin—the cabin of my parents. I wake to the wild, sad call of the loon. I listen to the call as the loon lands from flight in the crystal-clear waters of Eel Lake. I see His amazing beauty. Green feathers shimmer in the sunlight—I realize the loon has returned.

This magnificent loon has lived on Eel Lake for decades; this summer the loon cares for young ones with two chicks snuggled on the back of the female loon. I am thrilled with wonder. The chicks have faith, a total faith, that their female and male loon will protect them from the bald eagle and from the great horned owl.

The bald eagle and the great horned owl have lived on the lakeshore for decades, as well. I see them as I paddle in my canoe. The eagle soars above and the great horned owl is perched above. I trust, understanding the patterns of nature in the beauty all around me.

When I look left, my eyes spot the turtles on the log nearby. The reflections are clear; they safely sought bathing in sunshine upon an ancient log. Long grasses shield the turtles. It is spring-time once again, and they know what to do. Next summer, I will surely view more turtles on the old oak water-soaked log.

I am drawn to a white water lily in my direct frontal view. The lily speaks to me, as I softly paddle in the calm, peaceful lake waters.

Shadows of pine trees engulf my canoe. A large bass leaps in front of my canoe.

To my left I view another pure white water lily—resemblance of Christ? His blood was shed for me. My parents told me so, my teachers told me so, my pastor told me so, and my Bible school teachers told me so.

I remember the verses of the Bible; I remember the songs I sang—everyone one of the songs,

I was taught and sang; I remember.

This is how God speaks to me every day. "Jesus Shed His Blood for Me."

—if you can imagine—

Hoekstra-Van Ooyen Cabin

Golden Canoe

Eel Lake

Eel Lake

Reflection—Eel Lake

Nesting Loon

Eel Lake

Life—HOPE

Reflection

Evening Loon Reflection

Gifts

Cross Over

I will be going home. Upon the horizon, I see the bridge. I cross over, as I view flowers of many colors; I view unique designs, I hear the call of the birds, and watch the eagle in flight. I reminisce, I ponder, as a female loon glides beneath my canoe.

    Humbly, and quietly I move forward. I see all that my God has given me to see.

Divine encircles me
I understand
I love

"I Love You Lord"
"Be Still My Soul"
"I Rest in You, O Lord"
"Peace Be Still"
"And May the Lord Be with You"
"Great Is Thy Faithfulness"
"When the Roll Is Called Up Yonder"
"It Is Well with My Soul"

Peace

—if you could only imagine—

Immigration and assimilation will continue to be a struggle in the United States because we are a nation of immigrants.

On Golden Pond

Transition

River of Life

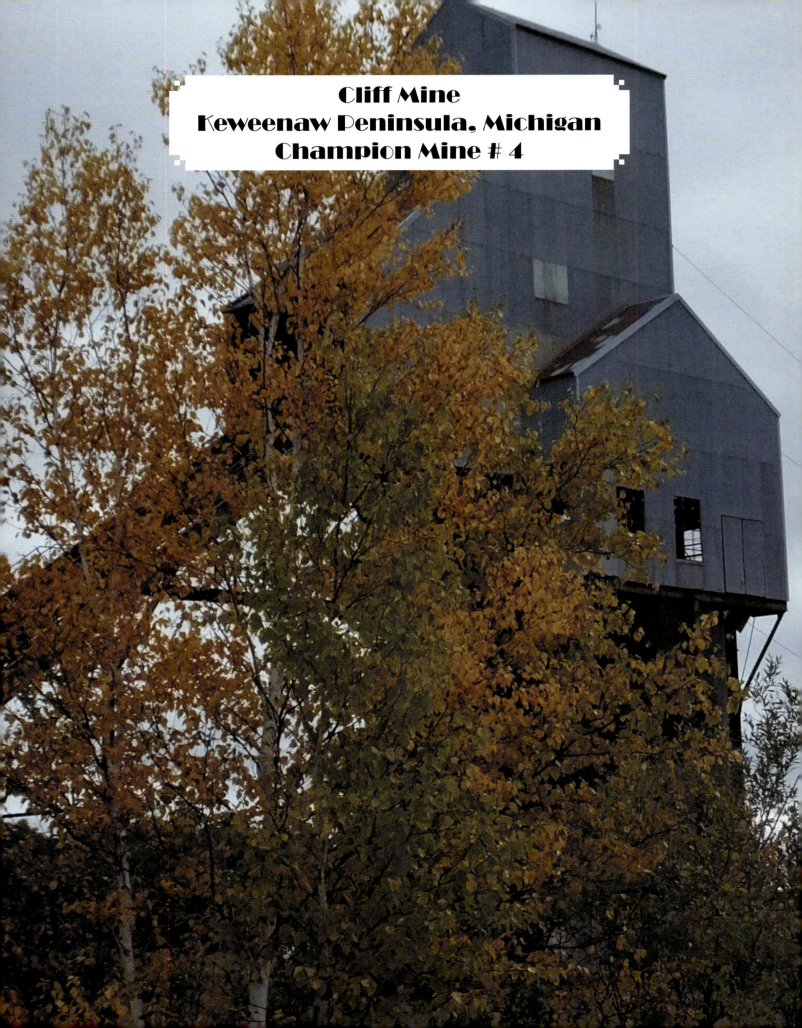

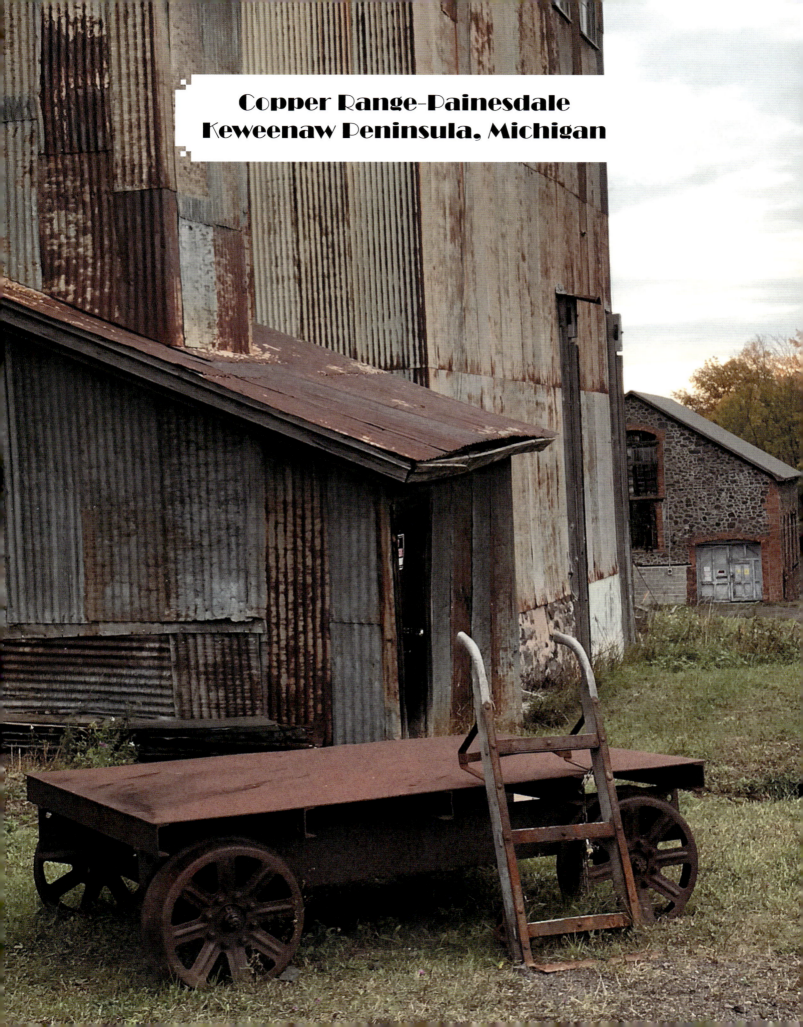

Quincy Mine
Upper Peninsula

Pure Copper

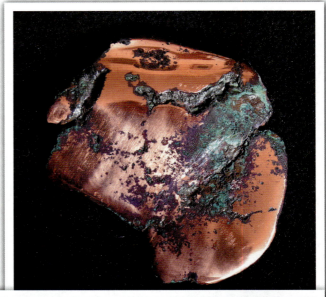

Lake Superior Shoreline Keweenaw Peninsula

Great Horned Owl

My eyes lift upward
I listen as I view
The sound of birds above
Drawn into my ears

My eyes view colors of green
Among and below the trees I lay
Bird calls become clarity
I hear the Cardinal

The call of the Goldfinch
The caw of the Blackbird
The tap of the Downy Woodpecker
The loud distant tap of the Pileated Woodpecker

The evening call of the Loon I hear
Bullfrogs sound their desperate evening croaks
High above, the Nightingale sooths my soul
After the clock strikes twelve

I tune in to the wisdom of the Great Horne Owl
I have returned
I hear the Great Owl speak
Wisdom is given

Imagine this story as yours.

Epilogue

Forward and backward—the photos tell the story. A story of immigration; promises within the struggles, the heartache, the journey viewed among immense beauty.

The photos portray the promises; the story is Anneke's new life in the United States.

At the age of three, Anneke walked to school with sister Tineke holding her hand along the pathway of a canal in Friesland. St. Nickolas and Zwarte Pete entered Anneke's classroom. When asked by Zarate Pete if Anneke had been good, Anneke shyly nodded her head yes. Soon all the children of the classroom were in the hallway, running ever so quickly, to pick up the Appenuten that had been strewn on the hallway floor.

Anneke's pockets were filled.

In a "new world," the USA, at the age of one day before age five, Anneke finds herself walking down a pathway leading to her new school in the USA.

Shy and hesitant, Anneke observes the large oak door; Anneke views the lock, and the large brass door handle.

Anneke opens the door.

A new life unfolds for Anneke.

A journey of schools, barns, and houses of immigrants—the struggle and toil, will become a part of the viewer and reader, as the sentiment of immigration is captured. All within a delightful swirl of colors, found within the magnificent architecture and nature of Northern and Upper Michigan.

Enjoy the travel. Truly, this is a story of family.

Anneke Letitia Van Ooyen Crans

Anneke can be contacted at 2371 Barry Street, Hudsonville, Michigan 49426
Email: annecrans74ac1@gmail.com

Profile

Anneke Letitia Van Ooyen Crans

Anneke Letitia carries her camera with intentional curiosity.

    A two-story school in North Bessemer, Michigan, caught Anneke's view. Peering through a broken pane on a first-floor window, shooting a photo into the dark, gave revelation to two classrooms. Photos follow—the story followed; Anneke journeyed as an immigrant.

    Photography is the focus; the story brings to life Anneke's childhood memories, and the life of first immigrant settlers in Upper and Lower Peninsulas of Michigan.

    In searching for detailed secrets within the schools, barns, and homes of Michigan—Anneke views the life and feels the joy, among struggles and pain. Anneke, a music instructor and photographer, captures the flow, captures the flow of beauty found within the structures of the past. Tonal colors of high and low permeate vibrations of life, as photos are viewed and the story is read.

    Anneke has been a winner in music performance and in her photography, where stunning beauty and design reveal hope and promise.

    Photographed and written in honor of Anneke's mother, Amy Joy Van Ooyen, author and naturalist, and father, Claude Peter Van Ooyen, musician and artist.

Acknowledgements

My life-time friend, LaVerne Blickley, walked with me, encouraging, engaging and suggesting. We often sat at her summer home, an old Army bus converted, on their 76 acres north. A glass of pomegranate juice, lunch with conversation and thought was the agenda. She was the wise guiding presence in my work. It is hard to put in words how much I've enjoyed working with LaVerne.

William Blickley was my computer technician. He was always ready to update my 2007 computer –getting it to work for a bit longer. His patience and skill, with a final suggestion or two, was appreciated.

Weekly, my brother, John Van Ooyen, visited our home. A three-course dinner followed by his help: how to insert, how to add photos, how to save, an overall "How To" curriculum. John researched and provided answers, assisted with computer and technical help. I am forever grateful to my Asian-Korean adopted brother for his friendship and honesty.

My loving husband receives credit for his patience, his historical information, his gift for helping me find the right term and often a title for my photos. His eye for the unusual, his willingness to make yet another stop for one more photo, thrusts my gratitude into deep appreciation.

Eight years ago, I began to take photos. My journey for this book began with a dilapidated, yet not forgotten, school building of early 1900's. Shooting photos through a cracked windowpane, the discovery of the past became the present and the reality - the beginning of "Pictured Life."

The Grand Valley Arts and the River City Camera Club artists became my mentors and inspiration, as I listened, and I learned, and I remained encouraged.

Many thanks to the excellent team at Archway Publishing, from Simon and Schuster:

Aimee Reff - Publishing Consultant, Deena Capron - Concierge, Kelly Wilson – Editorial Consultant, Kira Axsiom - Editorial Services Associate, Aaron Hurwitz – Marketing Consultant, Brad Wilhelm - Book Consultant, Reymond Mendez – Interior Designer, Jessica Busby – Cover Designer. Deena Capron was available for any question throughout this exciting process. She reviewed every step and often gave me suggestions on how to improve "Pictured Life."

The supportive team of Archway Publishing gave continual inspiration and helpful comments as we progressed through the development of "Pictured Life:"

"We look forward to working with you!"
"Attached is a Step-by Step Guide which outlines our process and timelines."
"I am pleased to deliver this proposal for your rewrites."
"Your document has been completed. Congratulations on reaching this milestone in your journey toward publication!"

Thanks to my many friends for their comments, encouragement and interest. You each have been my Inspiration!

Anneke Hoekstra Van Ooyen Crans

Anne Crans

Acknowledgements

Bessemer Library—Historical Information, 1938 snowstorm.

Blickley, LaVerne—Editor. "Recommendation."

Blickley, William—Computer tech, review. "Reflections."

County Offices of Ontonagon—Historical information. Ontonagon, Homestead, "Poor Farm."

Crans, John Donald—Advisor.

De Vries Doug - Vehicle photo identification.

Gayan, Lee and Tom—Historical facts. Ironwood, North Bessemer School.

Harmon, David—Historical information. Ironwood, North Bessemer School.

Hoekstra-Van Ooyen, Amy Joy—My Mother—in honor of her deep faith and fortitude.

Johanson, Bruce—Historical information. Ontonagon, Homestead, "Poor Farm."

Marin, Mary—Initial Book format.

Oppewal, Donna—Encouragement/advice.

Sell, Earle, Author and historian—Iron-Ore Mine map. Permission granted for inclusion by his son, Gary Sell—promotor of his father's work.

Strong, Tom—Historical information. Ontonagon, Homestead, "Poor Farm."

Timmer, Hubert – "Recommendation"

Rydzinski-Geyer, Suzanne—Hedberg History (Family Tree), North Bessemer School, Hedberg Farm, historical information.

Van Ooyen, Claude Peter—My Father, his creativity, his music, his quiet devotion.

Van Ooyen, John—my brother, Computer Tech.

Thank-You Ode

"Hand in Hand in Unison"

Red-Headed Woodpecker
Dazzling Yellow Goldfinch
House Wren
Minds arrange

Cedar Waxwings
Sandhill Cranes
Hummingbirds
Frogs

The Chorus has begun
"Pictured Life" is complete
Stories, poems, and photos
Past, present, future

A process
Unforgiving
The process
Giving

Friendship
Understanding
Communication
Complete

A million thanks,
To My Editor and Friend
LaVerne Blickley,

Anneke

Poems

Great Horned Owl
The Light Welcomes You
The Children
Do Not Cry
American Indian
Colors
Promise
Immigrants
Awe
Hope
Purpose
Indian Maiden
Great Horned Owl
I Listen

In Respect: Suzanne (Rydzinski) Geyer—Hedberg Family

I Listen

1912 Second Immigration
Stories spoken
Stories heard
Stories lived

Seven children
Crossing the Atlantic
In the corner
Not forgotten

The storm
Boat rocking
Porridge spilled
Porridge not tasted

Landed
Traveled West
Miles
Upper Peninsula

Michigan
Corner
Fields
Tree planted

The Apple Tree
The Grape Vine
The Raspberry Stem
The Maple Tree

Planted
Home Country
Finland
Fertile land

Left behind
New Land
Fertile land
Trees planted

Hope
Family of twelve children
Six daughters
Six sons

Home
Father the watchmaker
Mother the farmer
Children the helpers

Finn School
North Bessemer School
Wisdom of the Owl
Testimony

1902 First Immigration
Illinois
Finland return
USA return

Suzanne
The voice
The Family
Suzie

Hope

Suzanne (Rydzinski) Geyer is the granddaughter of Ida and Andrew Hedberg; solo living family member, owner of North Bessemer School and 120 acres on the corner of Hedberg Road and Simone Road. Suzanne purchased the school in 1972. Suzie's dream goal is to have the 120 acres be a respite for abused and abandoned animals.

Driving by North Bessemer School, I chanced to meet Suzie feeding her Holstein steers. Suzie brought cows back to the farm of her grandparents, knowing they "are watching from above."

One more view. I smile.

"If Only You Can Imagine"

Reflection—William Blickley

When I was reading your book and admiring the photographs, I was moved by the historicity of it.

I could feel the emotions of the little girl describing her experience. It must have been much like my grandparents from the Netherlands experienced. The "pastness" of the land and of the building photographs in the story is very moving. It made me think about the many people who struggled in this new land. It made me constantly think about the African Americans who still struggle to survive in this country. It reminded me that little African girls and boys whose parents had been captured from their homeland and taken here against their will, abused and alone, must have felt so much more lost and afraid. You clearly described of how foreign and threatening it felt, and what a struggle it was for your family getting settled in this land, coming prepared with supplies and friendly contacts here to help.

It is an emotional experience to read the narrative and to reflect on the photographs of the land and the articles of the past.

Impression—Blizzard—Hubert Timmer

My great-grandfather was one of those who were caught in the Blizzard of 1938 He had walked down the road to our relatives and was ready to leave for home. They cautioned him to stay back, and not go home as there was a snow-storm outside with blinding blowing snow and very low temperatures.

(I think the weather bureau data has it at (minus-fourteen degrees below zero.)

Being a Dutchman, he went ahead to beat the blizzard. Later he was found, almost home, frozen and buried in the snow drifts. *Pictured Life* brought back many memories of family life in the area.

Index

B

Bald Eagle 41, 175
Barns 67, 84, 167
Beppe 38
Bessemer Courthouse 170, 171
Blue Dodge Charger 103

D

Dr. Van Riper 52, 54, 55

F

First Settlers 31, 69, 80, 87, 100, 128, 135, 136, 160

G

Great horned owl 3, 175

H

Homestead 60, 66, 95, 99, 143, 144, 147

I

Implements 49
Indian Maiden 161, 162, 201

L

Loons 41, 43

N

North Bessemer School 1, 14, 15, 16, 17, 22, 23, 24, 202, 203

O

Ontonagon 142, 143, 144, 147, 199
Orange-belted bumblebee 34

P

Pake 38

R

Red Rose 38, 39, 94

S

Supplies 118, 204

Y

Yellow bumblebee 85